Lessons of Ulster

Lessons of Ulster

T. E. UTLEY

London

J. M. Dent & Sons Ltd

First published 1975
© Text, T. E. Utley, 1975
All rights reserved. No part of this
publication may be reproduced, stored
in a retrieval system, or transmitted,
in any form or by any means, electronic,
mechanical, photocopying, recording or
otherwise, without the prior permission
of J. M. Dent & Sons Ltd.

Made in Great Britain
at the
Aldine Press, Letchworth, Herts
for
J. M. Dent & Sons Ltd
Aldine House, 26 Albemarle Street, London

This book is set in 11 on 12pt Garamond 156

ISBN 0 460 04265 3

Contents

To Brigid

'The people of Ireland are not such damned fools
as the people of England . . .'

Lord Melbourne

Author's Foreword

This is not a history of the recent troubles in Ulster, but a critical study of one crucial and illuminating aspect of British policy during the last seven years.

My absorbing interest in and profound affection for the Province owes nothing to family connections. I am an Englishman, and I did not begin to visit Ulster continually until 1967. As an historian, in the extended sense in which that expression is applied to undergraduates, I had early become deeply interested in Anglo-Irish affairs, for they constitute a large and decisive part of the history of Britain. As an old-fashioned Tory, I have that instinctive sympathy for the Ulster Unionist cause which until recently was, and must now again become, one of the strongest characteristics of that great party. When, as a journalist, I was charged in the late 'sixties with the duty of commenting constantly on events in the Province, it was with these prejudices and this sort of equipment that I approached my task.

It soon became clear to me that, in Ulster, the great, permanent questions of political philosophy—the moral basis of authority and of the right to resist authority, the relationship between law and force and that between nationality and political allegiance—were being debated. It also seemed to me that, in some degree at least, the tragic conflict in Ulster might turn out to be a rehearsal for an even more devastating challenge to authority on this side of the Irish Sea. Finally, it seemed to me that successive British governments from the late 'sixties onwards were displaying, in their handling of Ulster, a degree of ineptitude which suggested not merely ignorance of Ireland but ignorance of the nature of politics itself. The Tory handling of Ulster, in particular, seemed to me to show clearly the decay of a whole tradition of political behaviour.

From all this I think there are general lessons to be derived, and this book is an attempt to point to some of them. It is a book about politics rather than about Ulster.

Since no book about politics can claim objectivity, the reader should throughout remind himself of my prejudices. I am a Unionist and, indeed, felt that conviction strongly enough to enter the political battle in Ulster as a parliamentary candidate at the General Election of February 1974. Nothing would delight me more than to see in Ulster a united society based on freely given allegiance, both Protestant and Roman Catholic, to the Crown. I am not that brand of Unionist, however, who thinks that there is any merit in denying the constant presence of potential conflict of allegiances in the Province, a conflict which from time to time becomes actual and acute. I also see no merit in simply saying that Ulster is part of the United Kingdom while the Republic is a foreign state, and leaving the matter there. The histories of both parts of Ireland, and of all Ireland with all Britain, are too closely linked to make any such simplification tolerable.

As to the method of the book, I have not set out to provide a narrative so much as an analysis. On the other hand, I have tried not to assume on the reader's part even an elementary knowledge of events there or of the order in which they happened. To prevent confusion, a short chronology of major events has been provided in the appendix.

The material on which the book relies consists almost entirely of personal observations, recorded in the course of innumerable visits to Ulster in the past seven years. For the opportunity of making these visits I am grateful to the *Daily Telegraph* and the *Sunday Telegraph*, as I am also for permission to reproduce some passages which have already appeared in those newspapers.

These often arduous trips, which I made as a feature writer and sometimes as a news reporter, would certainly have been impossible for me, a blind man, but for the constant help of my wife, who travelled with me and acted as my guide and amanuensis; and it is to her that this book is gratefully dedicated.

Obviously I cannot mention all those Ulstermen who, generally in the course of dispensing magnificent hospitality, have helped me to gain whatever understanding of the matter I have achieved. I cannot, however, omit to mention two of them—Mr Harold Wolseley, formerly the Royal Ulster Constabulary's City Commissioner for Belfast, who, in hours of delightful conversation, has taught me more about Ulster than I have learnt from any other single mentor; and Mr T. M. Roberts, Head of the Northern Ireland Information Service, whose friendship and counsel are among the chief boons which Ulster has to offer the visiting journalist. I have also had much valuable criticism and advice from Mr John Houston of the Conservative Research Department. It is a fair bet that none of these gentlemen would agree with everything I have written and none should therefore be held to blame for any of it.

In the preparation of the manuscript, I have had endless skilful and patient help from my gifted secretary and research assistant, Mary Dunlop.

TEU.
London, April 1975.

Chapter 1

Reflections on Ulster

In an immortal phrase, Miss Honor Tracy wrote, 'the Irish often complain that they are misunderstood; this is so and much to their advantage'.

There is, however, a reciprocal service which the Irish perform for us and the benefit of which is derived particularly by those British statesmen (and they are numerous in every generation) to whom it falls to play a part in Irish affairs. This service is to equip the British, who are uniquely proud of their talent for politics and in consequence peculiarly sensitive to the humiliation of political failure, with a 'problem' which is universally acknowledged to be insoluble and from the handling of which, however disastrously it may be conducted, nothing but honour can result. Ireland may be the graveyard of British statesmen, but it is also the highroad at any rate to posthumous glory. Those who plunge deeply into the Irish bog are revered for their courage and commonly exonerated from their ineptitude. If failure results from their exertions, the blame attaches to the Irish; if they achieve some semblance of momentary success (a few weeks' respite from violence, or the creation of a ramshackle coalition of incompatibles destined to collapse at the first impact with reality), they are praised for having appeased the unappeasable, clarified the inscrutable and generally demonstrated the superiority of Anglo-Saxon commonsense to Celtic lunacy.

In general, Ireland has come to provide a theatre in which, relieved of the immediate pressures of opinion on the mainland, British politicians are at liberty to indulge their weaknesses, exhibit to perfection the errors of the traditions in which they have been reared, and thereby to provide case studies from which invaluable lessons about the conduct of British politics can be inferred. The object of this essay is to elicit some of the lessons which have been supplied by Britain's handling of Ulster since 1968.

It starts from the outrageous and totally defensible proposition that Ulster presents nothing which it is particularly difficult to understand, that the forces which have been ranged against each other in this battle have, in relation both to their nature and their aims, been of an unusually comprehensible kind and that their behaviour (in particular, their response to British policy) has been peculiarly easy to predict. What has been displayed before us has not been some dark, complex, passionate scene compounded of black magic, but a straightforward conflict of easily defensible political ambitions. What we have brought to the settlement of that conflict is a grossly inadequate political equipment, a tradition full of errors about the nature of power and of politics, and a dedicated commitment to illusion. In this we have revealed ourselves in a manner which is important not only for the future of Ulster but for that of the whole United Kingdom.

Here, then, is a random selection of the vices and fallacies which, I maintain, have distinguished British policy in Ulster during this period. The dominant vice has been an obdurate refusal to recognize the existence of any ultimately and incorrigibly unpleasant fact. Positively, this has taken the form of an assumption that in politics there can be no final incompatible aspirations; that there is never a point at which it must be recognized that the wishes of one man are wholly irreconcilable with those of another; that there is never a dispute which can only be settled by force. This particular weakness bears fruit in one of the most cherished convictions of British liberalism—the belief in negotiation. Negotiation is seen not as a means of establishing where differences lie or even as a method of persuading adversaries to change their minds: it is seen rather as a form of therapy which, applied with however little regard to the nature of the disease or the character of the cure which it is supposed to effect, has an intrinsic virtue.

This, of course, is closely associated with another characteristically liberal assumption—the notion that politics presents a series of 'problems' to each of which some 'solution' must be presumed to exist. The idea is that this 'solution' will automatically emerge as a result of discussion round a table.

Closely associated with this is, of course, the fundamental view which lies at the very root of the liberal tradition, that the lawful exercise of force by the State is predestined to fail and will always in the end prove to be what is known in current jargon as 'counter-productive'. With tragic irony, this is combined with an inordinate belief in the efficacy of force when applied by rebels against the State.

This limitless faith in negotiation and boundless distrust of the efficacy of public force live uneasily alongside another characteristic liberal belief—the belief that Government has a moral duty to right the wrongs of history, to identify the underdog in every set of circumstances and to concentrate on the task of punishing his oppressors and redeeming his lot. This has also been one of the dominant themes in the story of Ulster since 1968.

Another of almost equal importance has been the obsession which has ruled British politics for several decades, the concept of 'the centre'. For a long time British politicians have found it convenient to postulate the existence at all times, and everywhere, of two sets of 'extremists', bereft of reason and humanity and single-mindedly devoted to mutual destruction and the annihilation of all who stand between them. The concomitant of this is the notion of 'the centre'. This is deemed to consist of the vast majority of mankind whose specific characteristics are held to be silence, moderation and a taste for compromise. When the search for such people proves unavailing (as if often does), British politicians seek to summon them into existence: this is an operation at which the British political genius excels. Thanks to the sovereign powers of the Parliament of Westminster over Ulster and the almost total economic dependence of that Province on Britain, it is one which, in this context, it has proved particularly easy to carry out with an almost total illusion of success. The method has simply been to induce certain Ulster politicians, cast in the mould of their fellow countrymen, to assume the demeanour and language which are favoured by moderate-minded people at Westminster. In the process, of course, these politicians have totally lost the support which they originally enjoyed in Ulster and have been rendered incapable of discharging the service for which they were employed—to deliver the Protestant majority. Nevertheless, the result has been a gratifying impression of successful British diplomacy. The irony is that, in the process, not only has something which might reasonably have been called 'the centre' been utterly destroyed in Ulster but a horde of 'extremists', who at the outset were latent or even moribund, have been conjured into militant activity. By this means, that polarization of Northern Irish politics which the British Government set out to end has for the first time been effectively created.

One of the chief conveniences of approaching politics with a set of automatic built-in responses such as I have described above is that it dispenses with the need for asking any fundamental questions. A rational man might think it prudent, before advancing an opinion about British policy in Ulster, to ask precisely what are the obligations which that policy must aim at discharging, and what are the interests which it is intended to serve. At any rate, these questions ought surely to have been considered by a Government which intended to mount a vast, costly and bloody military exercise in the Province. There is little evidence, however, of any clarity of thought by British politicians on these points. Certainly, they have never been frankly and exhaustively explored before the British public, save possibly in an occasional speech by Mr Enoch Powell.

The results of all this are striking. The British people find themselves embroiled in a quarrel, the origins of which are to most of them wholly obscure; they have little idea what purposes they are supposed to be striving for and no criteria by which to distinguish success from failure.

What is certain is that British Governments have both put in serious jeopardy the chances of maintaining the Union with Ulster, and made it virtually impossible to find a practicable, let alone an honourable, method of bringing the Union to an end should that be their intention. They have unnecessarily prolonged a cruel war within the United Kingdom, and have exposed to unprecedented danger a minority in Ulster which they set out to protect and to rescue. The only real hope which now remains of a tolerable conclusion of the matter springs from the fact that, by bloody and unnecessary experiments, almost all the alternatives to a sane policy have been exhausted. In all this there must surely be a message for Britain as well as for Ulster.

Chapter 2

British confusions

On the face of it, British policy in Ulster since 1968 may be thought to present no special problem of interpretation. Has it not been simply an outstanding example of one of the most familiar of all phenomena—the operation of British empiricism, the application of the well-worn rule that every question and every event should be judged on its own merits, plus the accompanying principle that in no circumstances should any abstract criterion of merit be set up? Have we, in fact, seen anything more remarkable than a series of well-intentioned efforts to cope with an intractable people, to act as an honest broker between contending parties, and to assuage violence by concession, and when that fails, to resist it with moderate and lawful force?

All this is true, but on a scale which makes other exercises in British empiricism look like instances of dogma and rational consistency run riot. What has been most conspicuous about policy in Ulster has been the total absence of any ultimate point of reference. It is not only that the policy has failed to provide any clear answers; it has failed even to formulate any intelligible questions. It has been bedevilled above all by being shaped under the influence of a whole host of mutually incompatible conceptions of the nature of Britain's relationship to Ulster, and therefore of the character of the obligations which spring from that relationship.

The simplest definition of that relationship is embodied in the oft-repeated statement that Ulster is 'an integral part of the United Kingdom'. Had successive British Governments, all of which have paid lip-service *ad nauseam* to this proposition, been prepared to act upon it, the consequences for British policy would have been plain and irresistible. The attempt to overthrow lawful government in Ulster by force would have been seen as an act of rebellion to be suppressed and punished as such. If it were thought that this act of rebellion sprang from social and political grievances which were remediable by law, it would have been seen to be the business of the Parliament at Westminster to remedy those grievances. This, after all, was well within its competence. Northern Ireland, it is true, had its own local Parliament, but such powers as it enjoyed were delegated by Westminster, which retained the right to legislate itself on all matters appertaining to the Province, and laws passed at Westminster, of course, took precedence over those enacted by Stormont.

The months spent by British Governments urging Stormont, by a combination of persuasion and menace, to introduce legislation for the protection of the minority and the establishment of what were described as 'British standards' are totally inexplicable on the premise that Ulster is simply a part of the United Kingdom. Had Westminster in fact accepted that premise, it could at any moment have set about the task of itself introducing any kind of anti-discriminatory legislation which it thought prudent. It could have done so, furthermore, without in any way altering the constitutional relationship between Stormont and Westminster.

Had British Governments simply proceeded on the assumption that Ulster was an integral part of the United Kingdom, their response to violence there would also have been fundamentally different. It is scarcely conceivable, for example, that in a state of civil disturbance in Britain large parts of Birmingham or Manchester would have been allowed for months on end to become rebel enclaves to which the police and the Army were denied access. It would have been quite incredible also that, at a time when the lawful authorities still had overwhelming force at their disposal, the leaders of a rebellion in Warwickshire or Lancashire would have been given safe conducts to London to discuss conditions of peace.

Ironically and absurdly, it was the status of Ulster as part of the United Kingdom which was most often cited as a defence for the weakness of security policy. The argument was that the citizens of a free nation could not be subjected to the rough sort of treatment which could properly be meted out to the subjects of a rebellious colony. The opposite is of course the truth. Where a state's credentials are in dispute, where it is applying force to subjects who are not represented in the shaping of its policy, where its functions are custodial and therefore—in theory at least—limited in time, it must tread warily, and it may be justified in doing business with its enemies. Where it is operating within its own domestic jurisdiction, on the other hand, and where the subjects it is trying to govern themselves constitute the source of its authority, then it cannot connive at breaches of the law or negotiate with those who challenge its sovereignty. Its business is government not diplomacy.

All this may seem obvious enough, but it suggests a fundamental question, the answer to which is crucial to any intelligent critique of British policy throughout the present crisis: why was it that the Parliament and people of the United Kingdom could not at any point bring themselves to think of or behave towards Ulster as though it were quite simply and without equivocation a part of the State? The geographical fact that Ireland is separated from Britain by a substantial expanse of sea is clearly part of the explanation. Added to this is the seemingly alien quality of Ulster's social and political life. Here, it seems, is a people whose life is dominated by conflicts which have long ceased to have the smallest importance in Britain. The impression that Ulster is engaged in a religious war, in a fight to the death about transubstantiation and the mediating role of the priesthood between God and Man, has probably done more than anything else to convince the ordinary British public that, whatever Ulster may be, it cannot be counted among Britain's domestic concerns. The essential truth is, however, that for the last half-century British opinion has, with almost total unanimity, classified Ireland as something more akin to a colonial than a domestic problem. This conception indeed was clearly written into the 1921 settlement. Paradoxically, it was proclaimed in the almost ludicrously impressive array of institutions with which the Province of Northern Ireland was equipped at the very outset of its existence.

Consider the origins of this strange sub-state: it was the by-product of a desperate attempt by British statesmen to reconcile the political aspirations of Southern Ireland with the determination of the Protestant population of the North to remain firmly and without qualification within the United Kingdom. The original hope was that both South and North would agree to accept Home Rule under the Crown. There would be separate governments in Dublin and Belfast, but these would be linked by a Council of Ireland which, it was widely hoped, might eventually lay the foundations of some sort of federal constitution. The possibility of such a settlement was removed when it became clear that the South would be content with nothing less than what was in effect dominion status. With the formation of the Irish Free State, Ulster was left with the governmental apparatus which had originally been intended as part of a Home Rule settlement for the whole of Ireland.

Ulster had never demanded this degree of devolution. In fact, it was intensely distasteful to Northern Unionists, and their leader, Sir James Craig (later Lord Craigavon), accepted it only as 'a supreme sacrifice', the price which the North had to pay for the maintenance of the Union with Britain. The upshot was a highly eccentric set of constitutional arrangements. The Six Counties of Northern Ireland continued to enjoy representation at Westminster—but on a scale far smaller than the size of their population justified.

They also had, however, their own Parliament, their own Government, their own Privy Council and their own Lord Chief Justice. Complicated financial provisions—which left all but the minimal taxing powers to Whitehall—made them effectively dependent for supply on the Parliament at Westminster, while at the same time concealing the extent of their own contribution to the coffers of the United Kingdom.

This dependence, however, was not resented. Initially, such resentment as there was was concentrated on the vast measure of unwanted autonomy which the settlement conferred. Stormont had virtually unlimited powers of legislation over domestic affairs, but it had little zeal for exercising those powers. Indeed, as time went on, it increasingly occupied itself in tamely reenacting for Northern Ireland legislation approved at Westminster for the rest of the United Kingdom.

There was only one sector of government in which Ulster came to value her autonomy. While she was willing to swallow whole the social and economic policies of successive British governments, she jealously guarded all those constitutional powers which she believed to relate to internal security. She maintained her own armed police force with its controversial B-Special Reserve, and her own Emergency Powers legislation which enabled the Executive to intern without trial. She retained her own control of the franchise for Stormont and local government elections—this last power was frequently employed to ensure Unionist majorities on local councils, and its abuse aroused righteous horror in the breasts of such English liberals as concerned themselves with the Province. It is impossible to understand these arrangements, however, without understanding the fortress mentality from which they sprang. In the early 'twenties, for example, three Nationalist-dominated councils had raised the tricolour, announced their intention of seceding to the Free State and started to send the minutes of their meetings to Dublin. It was not altogether unnatural that Unionists should take the view that the delimiting of local government constituencies had a bearing on the preservation of the State.

The point that matters in the present argument is that the sole merit of the Stormont settlement of 1921 in the eyes of the average Northern Irish Protestant was that it placed in local and supposedly responsible hands the rough and necessary business of defeating a conspiracy against the Union which, it was assumed, would be a permanent feature of Ulster's existence. In all other respects, devolution was distasteful to Ulster. In so far as the impressive array of political institutions with which the Province had been equipped acquired anything but a purely sentimental appeal, its value seemed to consist mostly in the fact that it guaranteed the control of the police to those who were resolved to maintain the Union.

From the British point of view, the value of the settlement was that it relieved British governments in normal circumstances from the irksome and embarrassing duty of governing directly the most turbulent area of the kingdom. So long as a firm understanding existed between British governments on the one hand, and the leaders of Unionist Ulster on the other, the arrangement achieved its principal purpose—the preservation of public order in the Province or, to put it more modestly, the avoidance of civil war. While the Conservatives remained the dominant political party in Britain this understanding was not hard to preserve. After all, they were essentially the party which stood for the unity of the kingdom and the party which was associated particularly with the cause of maintaining the authority of the Crown in Ulster. By the time the first Labour Government with an overall majority came to power in 1945, the terms of the partnership between London and Belfast were established strongly enough to put them beyond hazard, and Attlee's relations with Lord Brookeborough (Ulster's third Prime Minister) were as close as Baldwin's had been with Craigavon.

As conceived by the Left in Britain today, the partnership worked thus: a succession of Unionist overlords in Ulster (Craigavon, Andrews and Brookeborough), sustained by a perpetual Unionist majority at Stormont, quietly got on with

19

the task of maintaining the Protestant and British ascendancy in the Six Counties by means of the services of an armed police, a para-military auxiliary force and the recurrent use of the power to imprison without trial. The Nationalist Opposition virtually absented itself from politics in the Province, and the Parliament at Westminster was happy, so long as peace reigned, to refrain from all interference. The function of the British State in relation to Ulster was simply to provide an annual subsidy and the perpetual presence in the background of a military force which could (as, for instance, during the severe riots in Belfast in the summer of 1935) be swiftly and without controversy summoned to the decisive aid of the civil power.

This distorted picture contains elements of truth. A greater concern for Ulster in Britain during this period might have induced the Unionists in the Province to address their minds more diligently to the task of reconciling the Roman Catholic population as distinct from that of keeping the IRA (Irish Republican Army) in subjection. What is less often observed is another and far more serious effect of British detachment: this was to save British governments, the Parliament and the British people from the need ever to apply their minds to the harsh realities presented by the task of keeping peace in Ulster. Irish entanglements became simply a nightmare memory from the past, and when the time came again for British involvement, British opinion had nothing to bring to bear on the subject but a heritage of liberal illusions which are peculiarly irrelevant to the government of Ireland.

The crucial point is, however, that, when this juncture was reached, the complex constitutional relationship between Britain and Northern Ireland became a positive impediment to the cause of the Union. Here was a province which to all superficial appearances was independent, which had its own parliament and government and which had got itself, through its alien and incomprehensible ways, into a grievous mess from which it was now inviting Britain to rescue it. It was of no consequence that this account of the matter was wholly untrue, that, in strict terms, the sovereignty of Westminster applied to Northern Ireland; that devolution, however substantial, does not destroy the mutual obligations of the subjects of a kingdom; that the people of Northern Ireland paid their taxes to the Treasury, fought the Queen's wars and had, in respect of the majority of them, far less desire for separation or autonomy even than the

Scots or the Welsh. The appearance of the matter was totally different. Apologists for the Unionist cause have never realized the extent to which the existence of the Stormont settlement, with its overtones of independence, militated against the proposition that Ulster was, in a simple and straightforward sense, a part of the United Kingdom. The alternative view, that our obligations towards the Province were custodial, or in effect imperial, that we were there to hold the ring between contending factions and to preside over some sort of transition, was the one which most naturally occurred to the majority of the British people. It was also one which was naturally preferred by a Labour party which had come to recognize the electoral importance of the Irish Catholic vote and which, jettisoning Attlee's devotion to the Union, was now largely under the sway of the old radical tradition of support for the Irish underdog. The wisdom of those early Unionists, like Craigavon, who tried to stick out for integration and were profoundly nervous about the Stormont settlement, was to this extent thoroughly vindicated.

It was on the basis of a quite explicitly custodial theory of the nature of Britain's responsibilities towards Northern Ireland that Mr Wilson's Government took the decisive step of sending troops first to Londonderry on 13 August 1969, and then to Belfast on the 15th. A year of intermittent and increasingly serious rioting in the Province had culminated in a bitter battle in Londonderry which arose out of the commemoration on 12 August of the historic defence of the 'Maiden City' in 1690. Disorder spread to Belfast, where, it was generally believed, Catholic rioters had gone into action in an effort to relieve the pressure on their Londonderry brethren. According to the Scarman Commission which reported on 'Violence and Civil Disturbances in 1969', the pattern of rioting in the Province throughout 1968 and 1969 had been reasonably fixed. Civil Rights demonstrations, sometimes in defiance of public bans, had provoked fierce Protestant reactions. In Londonderry on 12 August, the fatal riot was sparked off by a normal and normally provocative Protestant procession which the authorities had thought it safer to permit than to forbid. The Catholics had taken the initiative in resorting to violence, and a ferocious conflict with the police, in which the Protestant demonstrators zealously participated, had ensued. In Belfast Catholic disorder had aroused a fierce Protestant reaction in the course of which much Catholic property had been destroyed. Casualties included a child accidentally shot dead by the police.

As the violence mounted throughout 1968 and 1969, both Stormont and the British Government had steadfastly taken the view that the Army should not be called in until local resources for the preservation of order had been exhausted. In pursuit of this policy, Major Chichester-Clark (Ulster's Prime Minister) had, on 15 July 1969, called the B-Special Reserve to the aid of the police who by the mid-summer of 1969 were virtually exhausted. This volunteer reserve, originally established by Mr Lloyd George's Government during the troubles of the early 'twenties, had been primarily intended and habitually used for the defence of the Border, and of military and civil installations against IRA infiltration and attack. Although its membership had never been restricted by law to Protestants, it was, by the very nature of its functions and the circumstances of its origins, a Protestant force. Its appearance on the scene, in the role of a riot control force (for which purpose it was not trained), was a highly emotive event. The RUC (the regular armed police force) was also predominantly Protestant in composition, though from the moment of its conception a genuine effort had been made to ensure that a third of its members should be recruited from the Catholic population. Both the main body of the force and its B-Special Reserve had been the butts of perennial criticism from Catholic politicians from the moment they came into being. This criticism had become intense, not to say wild, in the course of 1968 and 1969. Newspaper accounts and television pictures of the suppression of riots had created a widespread impression in Britain that the forces of law and order in Northern Ireland were brutal and irresponsible.

Later on in this book some attempt will be made to gauge the general validity of those criticisms. At present, all that it is necessary to say is this: the suppression of a riot by any police force in the world is an extremely ugly spectacle. The reporting of riots and the necessarily selective televising of particular incidents which occur in the course of the disturbance is a task which makes extreme demands on objectivity. It is part of the tradition of the press, which radio and television have fully inherited, and indeed substantially augmented, to err on the side of offering compassion to rioters and criticism to policemen. All the hostility generated towards the RUC and the B-Specials when the burden of restoring order fell upon them was promptly transferred to the

Army when that task devolved upon it. It may safely be wagered that had security operations in Ulster in 1968 and 1969 been in the hands of a force free of all historic suspicion and scientifically trained for riot dispersal, the balance of public sympathy by 1969 would have been against that force. As it was, there were historic suspicions in abundance; the RUC was deficient in up-to-date training for the suppression of riots, and the constant intrusion into the picture of Protestant hooligans, ever anxious to lend a hand to the authorities in teaching the rebels a lesson, ensured that public opinion on this side of the Irish Sea should be intensely hostile to the Northern Irish police.

All this contributed, then, to determining the character of the operations upon which Mr Callaghan as Home Secretary embarked in August 1969. They were seen not as an example of military assistance to the civil power but as an act of 'British intervention' in the affairs of an independent or semi-independent society over which Britain exercised, through her infinite misfortune, some kind of ultimate suzerainty. Indeed, the impression was formed that the 'British Army' (it was, of course, the United Kingdom Army) had gone to Ulster primarily to protect oppressed Catholics from their Protestant oppressors, or at best to act as umpire between contending factions equally fanatical and equally alien to the calm and practical ways of Britain. By natural association of ideas, it came to be equally accepted that the parallel function of the British Government was to bring about some political settlement in Northern Ireland which would enable the Province to sustain its own peace. Though imperial analogies in public speeches were discouraged, a growing tendency crept into the writing of commentators to treat Ulster in terms of those colonial crises with which the country had so often been faced in the process of liquidating its empire. Cyprus seemed to many to be a perfect illustration. Here, it was said, there were as in Ulster two nationalities with a tradition of mutual conflict. EOKA, with its demand for incorporation in Greece and its readiness to wage guerilla warfare to that end, seemed to be in some respects the equivalent of the IRA. The problem—that of reconciling the rights of two communities with an independent self-governing Cyprus—seemed at least to bear a close resemblance to that presented by Ulster.

So it was that when the troops had arrived and had been given a gratifyingly warm welcome by the Catholic population in some parts of Belfast and Londonderry, and had entered into practical diplomatic relations with all manner of street leaders (the heads of tenants' committees, citizens' defence committees and the like—people who were the self-appointed protectors of the 'minority' against the oppression of the authorities); and when a barbed-wire peace line had been set up designed to separate the Catholic and Protestant areas of Belfast from each other, Mr Callaghan paid a benevolent visit to the Province which set the tone and direction of British policy for many months. Its theme was that bluff British common sense was now to be brought to bear on the affairs of this distraught people. The old barriers of hostility and suspicion were to be swept away in a flood of *bonhomie*. Traditional enemies were to be brought together whenever possible in the same hotels and conference rooms and, when this was not possible, the avuncular Home Secretary would see them separately and act as go-between.

None of this involved any change in the constitutional relationship of the British and Stormont Governments. Indeed, the famous Downing Street declaration, which marked the beginning of the operation, was careful to emphasize that Stormont retained all its powers including its constitutional responsibility for security; but all the security forces were, in practice, to be put for the duration of the emergency under the control of the General Officer Commanding (GOC) Northern Ireland. General supervision of security policy was to be entrusted to a committee on which the Prime Minister of Ulster would sit with police and Army chiefs. A sort of ambassadorial representative of the British Government would provide a constant link between Whitehall and Stormont, and would in particular be charged with seeing to it that the Stormont Government carried out with promptness and fidelity a programme of reform designed to remove the legitimate grievances of the minority. The British were not engaged in a law enforcement operation only or even primarily; they were there to supply a 'political initiative'.

The theory on which this initiative was based became steadily clearer. It postulated that Ulster was divided into two extremes. The first was represented by the monolithic Unionist party which had enjoyed unchallenged power since the foundation of Northern Ireland. It had used that power, so it was said, to maintain an unqualified constant supremacy with the aid of armed force. It had also sought to preserve a monopoly of economic power. Jobs, always scarce in Ulster, had been given to Protestants rather than Catholics; and in the same way, houses had been distributed unfairly between the two communities. Since the oppression was built on the ascendancy of the Unionist party, the first object of the initiative must be to split that party up.

The troubles which had blown up in 1968 were in essence a protest by the Catholic population against its unendurable lot. They were inspired by nothing more sinister than the demand for elementary justice and 'British standards'. They had erupted into violence partly because of the ferocity with which these demands had been met and partly because, as was always the case, agitators and revolutionaries (not, at this moment, thought to have anything to do with the IRA) had rushed in to exploit discontent. A second object of the initiative, therefore, would have to be the separation of these extremists from the great bulk of moderate Catholic opinion.

All these interpretations had the merit of forcing the Ulster scene into a mould familiar and congenial to the English mind. British policy assumed the existence or at least the potential existence of a 'centre'—an amorphous mass of responsible, tolerant, silent and simple people ready to be mobilized in defence of compromise. The aim was to elicit and organize this 'centre'.

Spatial analogies in politics are always deceptive. Before it is possible to map out a 'middle way', it is at least desirable to know where the extremists stand. Had the main preoccupation of British policy simply been, as it was often said to be, to enforce 'British standards' in Ulster there would have been a perfectly simple way of doing this. It would have been to return to the original ambition of Unionism and incorporate Ulster unequivocally into the United Kingdom. As it was, the view prevailed that Ulster's difficulties could be solved within Ulster, though with the benefit of British guidance and custodianship as long as this was necessary. The notion that there lay at the root of those difficulties two totally incompatible aspirations— the aspiration of self-conscious political Catholicism in the Province towards Irish unity, and the aspiration of Protestant Ulster for some sort of indestructible safeguard against the danger that Irish unity would ever be achieved—was wholly excluded from British calculations. Instead, the British stubbornly clung as long as was possible to the theory that the quarrel in Ulster was purely and simply about civil rights. In the process, they misunderstood the natures both of Catholic and of Protestant Ulster, and succeeded in creating precisely that polarization which it was their declared object to end.

Chapter 3

Ulster 1969

The popular British view in 1969 of what Ulster was like was wrong in two fundamental respects. In the first place, it grossly exaggerated the extent to which the Province was socially divided. In the second, it both underrated and often mistook the identity of those forces which lay below the surface of the society in Ulster and carried within them the potentiality of civil war.

The first mistake was made plain in the continual use of the phrase 'the two communities'. This gave the impression that Ulster was virtually based on an oriental caste system, that Protestants and Catholics scarcely met each other save for the purpose of mutual combat, and that the Catholic community consisted almost exclusively of a poverty-stricken proletariat. In reality, the contact between Protestants and Catholics in the Province, and even the incidence of inter-marriage between them, had been at least great enough to create marked cultural differences between Southern and Northern Catholics. Some at least of the characteristics of what the British describe as the 'Scottish settlers' in the North have rubbed off on their Catholic neighbours. There is plenty of evidence also of the reverse process. Furthermore, the identification of the Protestants with the 'middle class' and the Catholics with an urban and rural proletariat was equally false. There was a substantial Catholic middle class, a vast Catholic peasantry and *petit bourgeoisie* and, of course, an enormous Protestant proletariat. The most serious impediment to contact between Protestants and Catholics was undoubtedly the strict educational segregation on which Catholics insisted, and which was a cause of offence to many Protestants. The State was obliged to acquiesce in segregated education, and indeed fell over backwards by generous subsidies to Catholic schools to ensure that it did not become a source of inequality. The professions were open to all religious denominations. In particular, the State had taken special care to ensure the appointment of a reasonable proportion of Catholics to the judiciary. Theoretically, the Civil Service was open to all Catholic entrants, although the proportion of Catholics actually employed in its higher reaches remained scandalously low, and there was constant controversy about the extent to which this was the result of Protestant prejudice or of Catholic reluctance to be involved in the administration of the State.

To quantify the extent of discrimination over employment in areas not controlled by the State is of course impossible. Economically, Ulster was and is a depressed area, and government never succeeded in eradicating the tendency to substantial unemployment, as endemic there as in the North-East of England and the other 'under-developed' regions of the United Kingdom. Sectarian discrimination was obviously more dangerous and more offensive because of the general shortage of jobs. Protestant employers were fully conscious of this, and it has for long been the custom of many of them to claim that they have always distributed jobs to Protestants and Catholics in a ratio of two to one, corresponding to the generally accepted view of the relative numbers of the two populations. On the other hand, impressive evidence exists that in many places this rule was far from being faithfully observed. There were also areas, like the shipyards of Belfast, which were virtually exclusive strongholds of Protestant labour. The argument normally used to justify these traditional Protestant preserves, particularly at moments of civil disorder and tension, was that it was merely asking for trouble to oblige Orangemen and Republicans to work on the same factory floor.

The same sort of argument no doubt often operated to prevent the promotion of Catholic workmen to positions of authority over their fellow workers. In all divided societies there are ample excuses for perpetuating discrimination; these excuses, however, are not always fraudulent. No doubt it would be ideal if all political and sectarian considerations could be ignored in distributing jobs in Ulster; anyone who supposes that this ideal could have been achieved at any moment in the past, or is likely to be easily achieved at any moment in the future without grave danger of public disorder, is profoundly foolish. It is just as foolish to underrate the practical difficulty of actually proving cases of discrimination, a fact which may render much of the anti-discriminatory legislation which has recently been imposed on the Province valuable mainly as an expression of principle. Segregated education, for instance, makes it possible to establish, without any intrusive questioning, what a man's religion is by simply asking him where he went to school.

More serious and concrete charges of discrimination, however, were made against the State itself. The Catholic population, of course, enjoyed the full benefit of the United Kingdom's Welfare State, and Protestants were never slow to point out the advantages which this gave to Ulster Catholics over their brethren across the Border. There were other areas of policy, however, in which it was said that Stormont showed flagrant discrimination in the allocation of the resources at its disposal. It was said, for example, that the new town of Craigavon, with all the employment opportunities which went with it, had been deliberately sited in a Protestant region when there were stronger arguments for putting it elsewhere. The argument was highly technical, and the O'Neill Administration rebutted it by pointing out that the siting of the town had been settled by an unimpeachably impartial commission. There was equally fierce controversy over the decision to put the new University of Ulster at Coleraine rather than Londonderry. Whatever the merits of that decision at the time it was taken, it does not seem in retrospect that Londonderry during the late 'sixties and early 'seventies would have been the most suitable possible spot for an academic grove.

The British imagination was more powerfully struck, however, by the charges relating to discrimination in local government. Although Stormont had followed the example of Westminster by copying, in its own electoral system, the reforms embodied in the Representation of the People Act, 1948, it had not reformed local government. There the franchise was confined, as it had been in England until 1948, to ratepayers. Furthermore, the demarcation of local government constituency boundaries, which had not yet been entrusted to an impartial commission but remained solely the responsibility of Stormont, provided the occasion for shameless gerrymandering, of which the classic example was provided by the arrangements made in Londonderry to ensure that a predominantly Catholic city should remain under perpetual Protestant control. The demand for 'one man, one vote' raised by the Civil Rights movement in the late 'sixties did not only have the merit of telling simplicity. Since no one in Britain knew to precisely what it referred, it subtly conveyed the impression (widespread even among the relatively sophisticated on this side of the Irish Sea) that the Catholics of Ulster were actually and statutorily disfranchised. The real issue was the propriety or otherwise of confining the right to elect local councillors (not of course Westminster or Stormont MPs) on a property qualification. Non-ratepaying Protestants were, of course, as much 'disfranchised' as non-ratepaying Catholics. The argument that this was a measure of sectarian discrimination (an argument which it was not commonly thought necessary by the Civil Rightists to spell out) ran thus: because of the economic inferiority of the Catholic population, the proportion of Catholic ratepayers was smaller than that of Protestant ratepayers. Catholic households were also commonly larger than those of Protestants. Accordingly, a ratepayer's franchise discriminated against Catholics and, taken in conjunction with the gerrymandering of constituency boundaries, ensured that Catholics were grossly under-represented in local government.

Thus stated, the argument is irrefutable. It leaves open, however, the question of how important a right is full representation in local government. To judge from the overwhelming apathy which local government elections normally arouse in all parts of the United Kingdom, it might seem that a local government vote does not rank high in the priceless heritage of British liberty, and that the lack of such a vote is certainly not an adequate reason for starting a revolution. This leaves out of account, however, one consideration which occupied an important part of the Civil Rights case. In Ulster, as in Britain, the responsibility for allocating houses rested with the local authorities, and it was alleged that there was constant and serious discrimination against Catholics in the distribution of houses.

The Cameron Commission into the causes of social disorder in the Province from 1968 upheld this allegation, but also put it into perspective. It quoted one glaring instance of discrimination which stuck in the memory—the case of a Protestant council which, while it had a long waiting list of large Catholic families, had given a whole house to a single Protestant girl. The councillor's explanation—that he was in effect rehousing her family who lived in very poor conditions, and that he had expected her to get married before she took possession (in fact she married shortly afterwards)—did not seem adequate to Cameron. As the Report put it: 'By no stretch of the imagination could Miss Beattie be regarded as a priority tenant.' However, the Report did not attempt to quantify discrimination, and it made the point that

Catholic councils showed exactly the same sort of preference for co-religionists.

In short, there is evidence and to spare of discrimination in Ulster before the present troubles began; but the extent of that discrimination was neither as great as was generally supposed in Britain, nor was all of it a kind which enlightened legislation could have swiftly removed. Emphatically, the Province was not divided into two entirely separate and mutually hostile 'communities'. Sectarian discrimination receives no recognition in the Province's laws or institutions. When later investigated by an independent Ombudsman, the Stormont Civil Service was awarded compliments which would have gratified the British Civil Service. The gravamen of the case against Northern Ireland's political institutions applied almost entirely to local government. The argument that the Protestant community held a monopoly of economic power was also ludicrously overstated. The main complaint of informed Marxists about Ulster, in fact, was never that the Protestants were rich and the Catholics poor, but that Protestant and Catholic workers were so misguided, and such credulous victims of capitalist propaganda, as to allow themselves to be diverted from their common struggle against the *bourgeoisie* by ancient and irrelevant political and sectarian quarrels.

What was certain was that until 1968 the factors which make for division in Ulster had been steadily declining in importance, and Ulster society had been becoming steadily more cohesive. Ulster had participated in the general increase in prosperity which marked this period throughout the United Kingdom. The Unionist Government of the Province, always given to interventionist economic policies and lavish with State support for trading and industrial ventures, had redoubled its efforts to find markets abroad and attract investment to Ulster. The Province also reflected all those secularizing influences which had gained such momentum in Britain. Churchgoing, and with it sectarian zeal, was declining, though not of course on the dramatic scale which had been visible in Britain for many years. The Province had its own rather tardy and often somewhat macabrely self-conscious imitation of 'permissiveness'. The miniskirt, for example, made a belated appearance, and in sophisticated suburbs and among the students at Queen's Belfast there was much excited talk (though generally only talk) about the advanced practices which were being introduced on the mainland.

Above all, the perennial enemy of the Union, whose constant presence had been the chief justification and up to a point the chief cause of the 'fortress mentality' of the Ulster Protestants, seemed to many to have been wiped out. The last sustained IRA campaign, confined largely to the Border areas and directed almost exclusively against installations and the police, had collapsed in utter ruin in 1963. It had been defeated by the almost unanimous hostility of the Catholic population of the Province, the relentless denunciations of the Catholic hierarchy and the resolute opposition of the Dublin Government, which had used internment freely for the purpose. The constitutional Catholic Opposition, supplied by the Nationalist party, was also becoming markedly subdued, and even constructively prepared to play its part in the proceedings at Stormont, from which it had so often absented itself. Its leader, Mr Eddie McAteer, agreed in February 1965 to accept the title of Leader of the Opposition.

The Unionist party kept, of course, its inevitable majority at Stormont, but from 1963 until 28 April 1969 that party was presided over by the most liberal leader it had ever had—Captain Terence (later Lord) O'Neill. Brought up partly in Abyssinia and partly at Eton and in the Brigade of Guards, he suffered from the first from a certain lack of contact with the more earthy elements in Ulster Unionism. His hereditary credentials as a re-conciler, however, were impeccable. Though a member of the Protestant ascendancy, he could also claim Gaelic roots. He brought to his task a wider knowledge of the outside world than any of his predecessors, and a taste for bold gestures and a capacity for eloquent speech which sharply distinguished him from them. In the end, Ulster Protestants were to become almost unanimous in condemning him, and the candour which he always showed in describing the faults of his colleagues no doubt explains much of this revulsion. The fact remains, however, that for a while O'Neill's achievement was remarkable. He set the Unionist party firmly in the direction of reform; he enlarged the terms in which the politics of Ulster could be discussed; he showed a strategic vision which, at the time, singled him out from all his colleagues, although in the end it was to be vitiated by his tactical blindness and by a taste for glamorous, presidential politics which was totally out of tune with the tradition of Ulster. This was illustrated particularly by his grandiloquent style of oratory and his addiction to foreign travel on a scale more appropriate to a Head of State than to the Prime Minister of a subordinate government—examples of these characteristic tendencies abound in his autobiography.

For a while, however, O'Neill seemed set fair to succeed. The new spirit was signalized by photographs of the Prime Minister consorting with nuns at convent prizegivings, by speeches which gave equal weight to the importance of building a united society and to that of preserving the Union, and, most daringly of all, by dramatic gestures of friendship towards the Irish Republic.

In 1965 O'Neill took the unprecedented step of inviting Mr Lemass, the Prime Minister of the Republic, to visit Belfast. With some justification, he later claimed this as the nearest approach yet achieved to exacting from the Government of the Republic, which still claimed a latent jurisdiction over the North, recognition of the legitimacy of Northern Ireland's constitutional arrangements. The visit was perforce arranged in a clandestine manner and with minimal consultation with his Cabinet colleagues. (See *The Autobiography of Terence O'Neill*, pages 68–73.) It caused a considerable uproar, but O'Neill got away with it, and it led immediately to a visit to Dublin by his Minister of Commerce, Brian Faulkner, and in the following year to a return visit by O'Neill to Lemass. These incidents show dramatically how close Ireland had come in the mid-'sixties to reconciliation. The Government of the Republic, though still theoretically committed to the view (written into its constitution) that it was the custodian of the rights and interests of the inhabitants of all Ireland, was almost wholly preoccupied with the task of converting Southern Ireland into a prosperous, up-to-date *bourgeois* community. Even Lemass's party, *Fianna Fail*, heir to *Sinn Fein*, the party which had refused to accept partition and maintained a bloody civil war against it, was now willing implicitly to recognize the existence of the North, at least to the extent of exchanging official hospitality.

What has to be explained is how, within two years of these events, Ulster was once again, to all appearances, on the brink of civil war. That explanation throws light on the second important misunderstanding about the state of Ulster which was prevalent in Britain at the time. Just as the extent to which Ulster was a divided society based on the hegemony of a Protestant master-class was absurdly exaggerated, so also the extent to which the traditional conflict over Irish unity had disappeared was dangerously overrated. Only just below the surface the old animosities survived. The historic conflict was nourished by regular ritual. Great anniversaries (the twelfth of July, which celebrates the Battle of the Boyne, and the twelfth of August, which commemorates the defence of Londonderry by the Apprentice Boys) continued to be duly celebrated, and the Hibernian Society continued to mount its annual Catholic procession. For the most part, these events were amiable occasions fully enjoyed by everyone, regardless of his cultural loyalty. From time to time, however, they would erupt into violence.

A famous and true story illustrates this state of affairs precisely. It concerns a Protestant lady in her seventies affectionately nicknamed (by virtue of her robust physiquê) 'Skinny Lizzie', who for many years kept a huckster's shop in Roman Catholic Hooker Street until it was razed to the ground by fire in a minor riot in 1968.

For 363 days out of every year, Skinny Lizzie enjoyed more cordial relations with her Roman Catholic neighbours than any decent Protestant in the Province of Northern Ireland. She was famous for her genial character and her facilities for extended credit. Yet she remained a woman of conviction. Each year on 10 July she would put up the Union Jack in preparation for the celebrations of the Twelfth. The higher echelons of the Royal Ulster Constabulary would visit her with earnest petitions to remove the offending symbol and even to take a few days' holiday in another part of the city until the Twelfth was over and normal civil life resumed. Invariably these petitions failed and the consequence was a riot of more or less severity.

Once rumour had it that her pet dog had been strung up on a lamp post; an investigation personally conducted by the Minister of Home Affairs at midnight was required to establish that the animal had died a natural death, otherwise there would undoubtedly have been Protestant reprisals.

The dynamite, then, was constantly present. The match was supplied by the emergence of a new political movement which, in its original character, was largely alien to the Ulster scene. To British eyes, the Civil Rights Movement which emerged in the late 'sixties was a moderate movement of liberal protest. Its programme—the abolition of the property qualification for local elections and an end to discrimination in housing and employment—seemed, by British standards, to be uncontroversial. That this programme should be fiercely resisted by the

Protestant majority in Northern Ireland was held to be a startling proof of how tyrannical that majority was.

In reality, the Civil Rights Association was from the first revolutionary in its ultimate aims, although it attracted a good deal of genuinely liberal support. Its first president was a Stalinist Communist, Betty Sinclair. In company with a number of her colleagues, she resigned as early as March 1969, because the movement was becoming too radical for her taste. She was succeeded by another Communist, Edwina Stewart. The Civil Rightists soon acquired a still more radical adjunct, the People's Democracy. This group, which soon grew to considerable proportions, consisted originally of a handful of students from The Queen's University, Belfast, including one Bernadette Devlin, who was destined, after her election to the House of Commons in April 1969, to be identified by British opinion as the authentic spokesman for Catholic Ulster. A prison sentence for her part in the Londonderry riots of 12 August 1969 confirmed this reputation. To the severest of her British critics, she seemed to be a gallant if somewhat naughty little girl. To the Left in Britain she was the Joan of Arc of Ulster. Her appearance in the Commons, at the age of twenty two and while still an undergraduate, provoked drooling sentimentality on all sides. After she had taken the oath, the Speaker was observed to hold her hand for an unusually long time, and Tories vied with Socialists in ladling out admiration for her. As time went on, her attacks on the British Army in Ulster as 'murderers' provoked in turn indignation and boredom, and the nadir of her Commons career was reached when, in January 1972, the House thought it not worth while disciplining her for a physical assault on the Home Secretary (Mr Maudling) in the course of Question Time.

In 1969, however, Bernadette Devlin and her associates had a firm reputation in Britain as the moderate representatives of an oppressed minority. The fact that their declared aim was the total destruction of the existing political institutions of both Northern and Southern Ireland and the substitution of a United Ireland Socialist Republic passed unnoticed. A modernist, secularist movement such as they represented certainly did not speak for any substantial sector of Northern Irish opinion, except in so far as it gave expression to a few and long-established grievances. Its historical function, however, which passed wholly unperceived in Britain, was to prepare the stage in Ulster for the triumphant re-entry of a traditional protagonist—

the IRA. The origin of the Civil Rights Movement itself was a private discussion in Londonderry in August 1967 at which Cathal Goulding, later known to the British public as the Commander-in-Chief of the Official IRA, was present. By 1972, the original Civil Rights Association, now denuded of its liberal elements, had become virtually indistinguishable from the political wing of the Official IRA; the People's Democracy in the guise of the Northern Civil Resistance Committee was virtually identical with the political wing of the Provisional IRA. The commonly accepted view that a fundamentally constitutional rule had been driven by adversity and oppression into extreme courses was almost wholly incorrect. In its purposes, the Civil Rights Movement was always revolutionary. Ostensibly it pursued those purposes by means of peaceful demonstration and passive resistance. It would organize sitdowns and mount demonstrations sometimes in defiance of the law. Unfortunately, its value as a civilian front behind which gunmen could go into action was quickly recognized by the IRA. A clash between 'peaceful demonstrators', whose aberrations could always be attributed to the unwanted presence of a handful of 'hooligans' in their midst, and the police or the Army, created perfect conditions for the activities of gunmen concealed in the crowd. As time went on, this pattern of violence became increasingly common in Northern Ireland until on 30 January 1972, on what has come to be known, in slavish obedience to IRA mythology, as 'Bloody Sunday', IRA exploitation of Civil Rights disturbances achieved supreme success—the creation of a state of mind in Britain favourable to the destruction of the Stormont Parliament and, thereby, the achievement of the first of the IRA's aims.

It is equally clear, however, that the Civil Rights Movement could never have achieved these astonishing successes but for the fierce reaction it elicited from Protestant extremists. This reaction, wholly incomprehensible in Britain, seemed natural and inevitable in Northern Ireland. Ulstermen knew that the conflict between the Civil Rights Movement and the authorities was largely a charade; that, just below the surface, the old gut conflict survived in the Province. On neither side was it seriously doubted that what was going on was a modern version of the old battle between nationalities, and the real issue was Irish nationalism versus Unionism. To militant Irish Nationalists, to the faithful remnant of the IRA, the existence of a moderate Unionist Government under O'Neill and the general trend of Ulster towards prosperity and reconciliation was a dire threat. Contrary to popular belief, maintained in the face of much historical experience, the danger-point in the affairs of any régime which is seriously challenged by a substantial number of its subjects, comes not when that régime is resisting all reform but when it has started belatedly on the path of concession. Had the O'Neill experiment succeeded it would have spelt death to Irish Nationalism. It would have created a prosperous and contented Ulster within the United Kingdom. The Catholic minority would have continued to pour libations on the graves of its martyrs and to sing patriotic tunes, but it would have settled down comfortably within the framework of the British welfare state. By the late 'sixties it had become urgent to counteract the lethal emollients of O'Neill. That was the task of the Civil Rights Movement. It provided a means of reviving the Nationalist cause.

The Nationalist minority, however, was not alone in being threatened by O'Neill's moderation. Protestant Ulster has always been divided between those whose main concern is the preservation of the Union with Britain, and those whose chief interest is in maintaining the Protestant supremacy. Among the Protestant working classes of Ulster, rural and urban, there has always been present a fanatical tradition of anti-popery arising not so much from religious conviction as from racial fear. The belief that, as a result of their breeding habits, the Catholic minority would eventually become the majority and drag Ulster into a Romish United Ireland could not be easily exorcised. On the contrary, it was fanned into fury by the spectacle of a Unionist Prime Minister visiting Dublin and giving away prizes at convent schools. There was much in the atmosphere of the 'sixties which was distasteful to the conservatism even of moderate Protestants. The decline of religious fervour, the painful birth of ecumenism and the import, gradual though it was, of trendy ways in manners and morals from across the Irish Sea, all prepared the way for evangelical revival which was bound to spill over into politics. The hour supplied the man in the shape of Ian Paisley.

In October 1956 the still relatively peaceful politics of Ulster were suddenly disturbed by a minor crisis; the bare facts of the matter were not remarkable. A fifteen year old Belfast girl, Maura Lyons, had quarrelled with her parents, been chastised by her father and run away from home. She was later discovered in England where, for several months, she lived in hiding and in

36

disguise, passed from hand to hand by a chain of anonymous benefactors.

What lent colour to the story in Britain, and explosive quality to it in Ulster, was that the source of the trouble was religious. Maura's parents were Catholics; she herself, having from her earliest years been attracted by the notion of one day entering a convent, had suddenly fallen in with the members of a relatively new Protestant Church, had begun to attend prayer meetings, and had last been seen in the company of a minister of that Church.

In the eyes of Republicans, her disappearance was a clear example of abduction of a minor by a highly organized and thoroughly unscrupulous religious sect. In the eyes of some Protestants, it was a proof of the intolerable oppression employed by Romish families to keep their young in slavery and superstition.

In the context of Ulster, the case was bound to have immediate political implications, and it was the subject of several debates at Stormont. Who, Republicans would ask, could be sure that a Protestant police force would do its best to protect Catholic parents from the ever-present danger of having their children kidnapped by Protestant clergymen? Who, extreme Protestants would inquire, could be sure that in these feeble modern times the State in Ulster would run the risk of political trouble to protect a helpless maiden convert to the Bible from the brutal reprisals of her parents?

In December, as feelings mounted, a vast concourse gathered in the Ulster Hall to be addressed by the head of the Free Presbyterian Church itself, a young preacher of rising fame and imposing stature, the Reverend Ian Paisley. He played to them what was widely accepted as a recording of the girl's voice (though some—including her parents—disputed its authenticity) announcing her conversion and explaining that she had fled from her parents of her own free will to escape incarceration in a convent.

Hymns were sung, prayers bellowed, and Mr Paisley declared that if he knew the girl's whereabouts he would not reveal them to the police, even if he had to go to jail. 'I will do time for it. I will be proud to do time for Protestant liberty.'

In the event, the offer was not taken up. On her sixteenth birthday, the girl landed up at Mr Paisley's house in Belfast. She was duly conducted by him and his solicitor to the police, who had meanwhile issued a warrant for her apprehension as a person in need of care and protection and, at the station, amid much weeping and recrimination, there ensued a characteristically Irish scene.

Her Aunty doused her in holy water and kissed her. Her father hit Mr Paisley's solicitor in the apparent belief that this gentleman had something to do with the girl's disappearance; but on discovering his error, he apologized, and the girl was packed off to a local authority home pending the hearing of her case.

The matter was eventually resolved by an order of the High Court making Maura Lyons a Ward and appointing her father, subject to certain stringent provisions concerning respect for her religious convictions, as guardian.

This story shows Paisley in a role which he occupied in the middle 'sixties. He was the leader of a fiercely anti-establishment movement; his power base, still predominantly working class, was provided by the remnants of that extreme Calvinistic tradition which had never been wholly eliminated from Ulster and which had always flourished in a few back-street chapels in the Protestant areas of Belfast. Paisley, who had been ordained by his own father, was the founder of a new evangelical Church describing itself as the 'Free Presbyterians'. He brought to his mission outstanding demagogic powers, a great organizing ability, a certain amount of training procured in the USA in the up-to-date techniques of evangelization, and a Doctorate of Divinity of more than dubious academic standing from the Bob Jones University in North Carolina. With the aid of this equipment, he established a highly successful Church which rapidly grew in riches and influence: through him, already widespread fears about new-fangled doctrines and the growth of popish practices found expression and he soon began to make quite serious inroads on the regular denominations.

The essential point is, however, that until mid-1969 at any rate, Paisley remained a peripheral figure, a perpetual nuisance to the authorities, and an object either of fierce scorn or amused ridicule to the vast majority of ordinary Ulstermen. In 1966, for example, he earned a three-month prison sentence for riotous behaviour in Armagh following a march against the General Assembly of the Presbyterian Church which he had felt obliged to chastise for Romish tendencies. His career of protest—against the Pope, the Archbishop of Canterbury and the Reverend Lord

Soper—won him a fair return in column inches both in Ulster and in Britain; but he did not become a formidable threat until the emergence of the Civil Rights Movement gave him an opportunity to carry his activities into politics. The vigorous part which his supporters played in obstructing Civil Rights marches and fighting Civil Rights marchers provided some of the most lurid items in television news broadcasts. The famous ambush at Burntollet Bridge (see Cameron Report page 92) on 5 January 1969, when Civil Rights marchers were brutally attacked with stones and sticks studded with nails now has a secure place in Nationalist mythology. What mattered, however, was that it was easy, particularly, for the British public to confuse the actions of Protestant rioters against Civil Rights marchers with the action of the police (which itself, at times, left much to be desired). The spectacle of these confrontations encouraged the view in Britain that what was going on in Ulster was not a conflict between the law and rebels but a conflict between two lots of fanatical thugs. By augmenting violence, Protestant extremists brought the O'Neill Government into still further discredit. Since the initiative in mounting demonstrations was generally taken by the Civil Rights marchers rather than by Paisley sympathizers, Protestant opinion in Ulster did not find it hard to reach the conclusion that the fault lay with a weak-minded progressive Government which stubbornly refused to recognize that the Civil Rightists were in fact the IRA in thin camouflage, and that the old battle had once again been resumed.

All this broadened the base of Paisley's appeal, and he ceased to be thought of as the leader of a quaintly fanatical body of religious traditionalists held together by the personal magnetism of an odd survival from the seventeenth century. Increasingly, relatively staid Unionists began to confess somewhat shamefacedly that, whatever might be thought of the Doctor, he at least was speaking out for Ulster and denouncing not only the traitors within the gates but the hordes of sympathizers they seemed to have across the Irish Sea.

In February 1969 Paisley achieved a moral victory by ensuring that in his own constituency, O'Neill was returned to the Stormont Parliament by only a minority vote. When O'Neill left politics in May, Paisley fought the seat again and swept to victory. At the Westminster General Election of June 1970, he won the hitherto safe Unionist seat of North Antrim from a liberal-minded representative of the Protestant Assembly, Henry

Clarke. There followed a Westminster career curiously parallel in several respects to that of Bernadette Devlin. Once established in the Mother of Parliaments, the dreaded Doctor began to win improbable friends. His colourful behaviour, carefully moderated to meet the requirements of Parliamentary convention, went straight to the hearts of many Parliamentary colleagues who love nothing so much as a stage Irishman of whatever political or religious brand. Many who suspected even O'Neill of representing only a more sophisticated variety of Protestant oppression found Doctor Paisley 'a good fellow', all the more refreshing for being a little out of the ordinary run. What is more, Paisley's relatively decorous behaviour in London gave the Commons a welcome opportunity for self-congratulation. Tory back-benchers would knowingly whisper that this wild Irishman had been tamed by membership of the greatest club in the world. This success strengthened Paisley at home; he won, it was said, more respect from the lily-livered British than did those Ulster politicians who fell over backwards to pander to British foibles and illusions. Only when, in 1973, Paisley, in spite of the mollifying influence of three years at Westminster, was seen at the centre of a riot in the newly created Northern Irish Assembly from which he had to be physically ejected by the police, did Westminster begin to resume its doubts.

What mattered in 1968 and 1969, however, was that the O'Neill Government found itself bitterly assailed from two sides. Repeated demonstrations led to violent clashes between Civil Rightists and Protestant extremists. An over-strained and under-manned police force occasionally and inevitably lost its head, and there were some proven incidents of police indiscipline on an inexcusable scale. The fact that an independent investigation established that the police 'certainly' showed none of the consistent complicity with Protestant rioters which was freely attributed to them, did nothing to redeem their reputation in Britain when this was eventually established. In facing these challenges, the O'Neill Government was subject to constant (although, by later standards, relatively gentle) pressure from Whitehall both to maintain a vigorous reforming policy and to refrain from any extreme reaction to disorder. In coping with the riots, the Government tried to steer a middle course between repression and pusillanimity. Sometimes it banned or rerouted marches, and sometimes it allowed them to proceed in the interest of the sacred right of free assembly. In either case, trouble ensued and the blame for it was visited on O'Neill. Not until the beginning of 1969 did he muster the courage to bring in a fairly tough Public Order (Amendment) Bill. Much of his effort at the time was concentrated on convincing his Protestant critics that Civil Rights disturbances, regrettable as they were, had nothing to do with the IRA. In March and April, however, a new and sinister development took all the force out of his plea. A series of explosions at electricity and water installations bore, in almost everybody's eyes, the authentic signature of the IRA. In reality, this 'Popish plot', like its famous English predecessor, was mounted by Protestant extremists, confident that all that was needed to topple O'Neill was one convincing piece of evidence of IRA participation.

Meanwhile, O'Neill steadfastly pursued his reformist course or, to put it more accurately, sedulously fostered his reformist image. He passionately believed, and on the strength of some evidence, that although the extremists of both Right and Left occupied the centre of the stage, the overwhelming mass of Ulstermen were on his side. Increasingly, however, his political colleagues in the Unionist party were not. The growing internal dissensions in the Unionist party sprang not only from the Government's failure to re-establish order but also from the increasing conviction that O'Neill—his personality no less than his policy—was an actual incitement to disorder. The actual content of that policy seems indeed in retrospect to have been remarkably thin. O'Neill is a classic example of the dangers of government by gesture. These gestures—dramatic speeches and appeals on television, for example, elaborate foreign tours, and overtures to the South and the Catholic minority—excited Protestant suspicion without materially reducing Catholic grievances. Before the end of 1968, he had felt constrained to dismiss his Minister for Home Affairs, William Craig, not for his handling of riots (for which he had been much criticized) but for a flamboyant speech in which he had suggested that Ulster, if need be, could dispense altogether with the British connection and set her own house in order without the aid of incessant counsel and criticism from Westminster. O'Neill was used to dealing with rebellions in the party with a combination of charm and patrician hauteur. Hitherto, vigorous reprimands had sufficed to bring the dissidents into line; but irritation, arising largely from the feeling that the Prime Minister considered himself to represent a level of sophistication far higher than that of most of his colleagues (he was an excellent mimic, and was fond of imitating the earthy Ulster accents of some of them) mounted to boiling point by the beginning of 1969.

In January, Brian Faulkner, the most formidable of those colleagues, resigned. He was already seen by many as the most talented politician in Ulster, but more important than that, he came of that prosperous Presbyterian commercial middle class, entrenched in Protestant virtue and sober loyalty to the Unionists, whose support was essential to O'Neill's success. That class, which still carried with it the deference of vast numbers of Ulster working men and the trust of the farming community, had no great taste for rabble-rousers like Paisley; but it had no great taste either for aristocratic liberals with foreign ways, and it had begun profoundly to distrust O'Neill. Faulkner and O'Neill together might have saved Ulster. It is a criticism of both of them that trivial factors of personality and even social prejudice made their co-operation ultimately impossible. O'Neill was a direct and commanding man, and a romantic; Faulkner was calculating, not easily accessible to close friendship and given to the pursuit of political ends by oblique means. O'Neill belonged to the Anglicized and liberally inclined wing of the Protestant ascendancy; Faulkner was the personification of the middle class. Such distinctions in Ulster are much more vivid than in twentieth-century Britain; the stated reason in his resignation seemed to British eyes deceptively trivial. He opposed O'Neill's decision to appoint the Cameron Commission to investigate the causes of civil disturbances in 1968. It was generally assumed in Britain that what he really opposed was any substantial move towards political and social reform and more particularly the granting of universal suffrage for local government elections. In reality, Faulkner's position at the time seems to have been this: independent judicial investigations which appeared to put the authorities in the dock or, at best, to lay Ulster on the psychiatrist's couch would seem only like a victory for the rebels. In defending the law, the State must be self-confident and unapologetic. When it came to reform, the Government should act rather than talk, for talking provokes without placating. Faulkner was recommending a subtle recipe for the Government of Ulster—radical policies in a conservative idiom.

It was not surprising that a day or two after Faulkner's departure, the Minister of Health and Social Services, William Morgan, should follow in his footsteps. He went for some obscure reason that he was afraid of the effect of present policies on the country's economic future. Joseph Burns, the Assistant Whip, followed him.

Faced with these desertions and a dwindling majority at Stormont, O'Neill took the supreme gamble of calling a General Election which he hoped would mobilize the silent majority to his aid. Statistically, he was not far out: pro-O'Neill votes numbered 230,000 against 120,000 votes for anti-O'Neill Protestants. The resulting distribution of seats, however, left O'Neill as precariously poised as before. The continuance of violence, the allegedly IRA explosions and the persistence of dissent within the Unionist party destroyed him within three months. The *coup de grâce* was administered by another resignation, that of Major James Chichester-Clark. To all appearances the issue here was more substantial; after months of dilly-dallying, O'Neill announced the intention of his Government to reform the local government franchise on the basis of one man, one vote. Chichester-Clark, having appeared to acquiesce in this decision, rejected it on the ground not that it was in itself bad but that it was ill-timed. A kinsman of O'Neill but a man with far closer contact than O'Neill ever had with the roots of Ulster, and a simple country squire who farmed his own land and was credited with a distaste for politics, Chichester-Clark, like Faulkner, held the key to the loyalty of many Unionists; his desertion was a fatal blow. It led almost immediately to O'Neill's own resignation.

In British eyes Ulster politics had swung fatally to the Right; but the truth was more complex. Those who deserted O'Neill at this time were inspired mainly by the conviction that his leadership, quite irrespective of the policies to which he was attached, had become intolerable, and the feeling was that a change of Prime Minister would itself be as good as a tonic. It was comforting to take refuge in the view that what had suddenly transformed Ulster from a peaceful and contented society into a bear-garden was nothing more fundamental than the vanity and tactlessness of one man.

The error of that view was soon tragically clear. In essence, the criticism of O'Neill was that he had failed both to suppress disorder and to disarm it by concrete concessions. A resolute, quietly conducted policy compounded of coercion and reform could, it was said, have averted catastrophe. Up to a point, that criticism stands. Where it fails, however, is that it underrates

43

the constricting limits within which O'Neill had to operate. The chief of these was the British Government's insistence that nothing but reform was required to restore peace in Ulster. The total misunderstanding in Britain of the revolutionary character of the Civil Rights Movement, and the consequent misunderstanding of the strength and dangerous potentiality of the reaction which that movement provoked, made sensible policies in Ulster almost impossible. The only physical resource available for the reinforcement of the police, for example, was the B-Special Reserve; it was never intended for use in the suppression of riots and it had already been falsely identified in Britain as the chief instrument of Protestant oppression. Had it been called out in 1968 or early 1969, the British reaction would certainly have been extreme.

The irony is that at the beginning of 1968 the centre was in power in Ulster in the shape of a Unionist administration far more liberal than any which had preceded it. The country was advancing in prosperity and moving towards reconciliation; the forces which challenged this progress were peripheral and largely subterranean. In its search for a centre in Ulster politics, Britain helped to destroy that centre which already existed. In the process, she strengthened, by crass misunderstanding, everything that was making for division in the Province.

Chapter 4

Chichester-Clark

Seen from Britain, the events leading up to the dispatch of substantial UK military forces to restore order in Ulster in August 1969 were clear enough: a rigid, tyrannical Protestant majority was refusing legitimate demands for liberal reform. A Catholic minority, exasperated beyond the point of endurance, was seeking to secure reforms by popular demonstrations which, because of the inevitable activity of hooligans, sometimes became violent. A Protestant rabble, operating with the partial connivance of the authorities, was reacting furiously against these demonstrations and setting the scene for civil war.

On this view, the resignation of O'Neill and the succession of Chichester-Clark represented victory for the Right. O'Neill, though not sufficiently energetic for the tastes of the British Left, had at least set off on the path of reform. Chichester-Clark, it was commonly believed, was a hard-liner who had plotted against him and could now be expected to set the clock back.

Seen from Ulster, the train of events was strikingly different. The case which was most widely urged against O'Neill was that he had aroused both expectations and fears by lavish promises of reform, while doing comparatively little to fulfil them. He had made gestures calculated to provoke Protestant anger without doing anything remotely effective to disarm Catholic protest. In the opinion of the more severe of his colleagues, he had stirred up trouble; they accused him of being a dilettante, and of lacking real contact with Ulster society. Moderate Protestant opinion, still baffled by the suddenness with which Ulster had been dragged to the brink of civil war at the very moment when it seemed that everything was set fair for progress and reconciliation, took refuge in the thought that if the mercurial, interfering O'Neill could only be removed, the natural course of history could be resumed.

For a short while after Chichester-Clark's succession, this

happy illusion persisted. The new Prime Minister was granted a period of probation even by Dr Paisley. Chichester-Clark had resigned from the O'Neill administration because he thought that the granting of 'one man, one vote' was premature; but he instantly made it clear that this crucial policy decision having been taken before his accession, he would not dream of trying to overturn it. He soon proved that he was at least as liberal as his predecessor. The difference was that he had a quiet, re-assuring manner and no taste for rhetoric. It seemed at least on the cards that he would be able to convince the Protestants that he was capable of re-establishing order while proceeding, without offensive flourishes, to remove fundamental minority grievances. He started his career by announcing an amnesty for all those who had been involved without grave criminality in the most recent troubles. Since the benefit of this amnesty was enjoyed equally by Dr Paisley and several eminent minority politicians, it seemed at the time a shrewd move, an indication that, after all this nonsense, Ulster, now under the commonsense leadership of a decent farmer, might revert to reality.

These hopes were short-lived, and the reason why is crucial to the argument of this book. It had certainly nothing to do with any reluctance on Chichester-Clark's part to maintain and in-crease the reform programme. On the contrary, this rapidly assumed the most impressive dimensions. Little more than three weeks after he took office, he was able to point out that a Bill for the establishment of an Ombudsman had already been introduced, that local government elections on a universal franchise were promised, that a points system for the allocation of housing had been drawn up, and that yet another Commission (the Cameron Commission) was to investigate the causes of disorder. As time went on, the programme was rapidly extended until it satisfied every one of the original demands of the Civil Rights Movement, equipping Ulster with legislation against religious prejudice and discrimination in employment, and giving her all the other hallmarks of an ultra-civilized modern state.

The extent of this programme, indeed, took the Civil Rights Movement by surprise and the Stormont Opposition itself felt constrained at one point to intimate that it was satisfied. Yet violence continued and intensified. Its pattern remained roughly what it had been in 1968: Civil Rights demonstrations evoked Protestant reprisals, Protestant demonstrations evoked

Civil Rights reprisals. Sometimes trouble was sparked off by purely local causes which had nothing to do with high principles of policy, but there were always to hand eminent men from each side of the community to advocate the cause of the rioters and to accuse the police of brutality in suppressing them. By now, the Civil Rights Movement was in total disarray. The moderate wing, under the chairmanship of a sensible Communist, favoured temperate policies, but the People's Democracy (a miscellaneous bunch of Trotskyists, Maoists, and sympathizers of both the Official IRA and the Provisional IRA) was rapidly taking the initiative. All the time it was sustained in the campaign by the moral support of British liberals who conceived that it represented roughly the political principles of Mr Gladstone and consisted of moderate constitutionalists whose natural habitat was the smoking-room of the Reform Club.

No matter what was conceded, the critics of the régime remained implacable. They were slow indeed to think up new political reforms, but they could always concentrate their energies on attacking measures designed to re-establish order. It was this which made the formula of reform plus the vigorous defence of the State for which Chichester-Clark stood hard to achieve. The truth was that Ulster was being assailed, in the most literal meaning of the phrase, by a 'subversive movement'.

Subversion is to be distinguished from revolution. A revolutionary movement aims at the achievement of certain specific ends: largely, the substitution of one régime for another. A subversive movement aims simply at the destruction of government and society in the belief that something better is bound to ensue. This represented precisely the spirit of the People's Democracy. By itself it could achieve nothing but the weakening of government. Consciously or otherwise, therefore, its role was preparatory: it was there to set the scene for the entry of the IRA. Some of its members knew and wanted this; others simply revelled in the task of attacking the Establishment. Many of them spoke in the most up-to-date idiom of Leftist expression, but what lent significance to their work was not the language they used and the concepts they espoused, but the traditional conflicts which they could exploit. In whatever terms the argument began, it was historically bound to end as a debate about Irish Unity. Inexplicably, this palpable truth was concealed from almost all British politicians.

By midsummer, the undermanned RUC, which had been

coping with progressively more furious street fighting, had reached a point at which, in the opinion of Mr Harold Wolseley, Belfast's City Commissioner of Police (an opinion subsequently upheld by the Scarman Commission), it was impossible for it to continue to discharge its functions without military assistance. One day in July, the civil power was indeed obliged to call on the aid of the local garrison, although troops were not in fact brought into action. The three-day riots in Londonderry, sparked off by attacks from the Bogside on the Apprentice Boys' procession, accompanied by diversionary riots in Belfast, conclusively proved Mr Wolseley to be right. The arrival in force of the UK Army in Londonderry and Belfast opened a new phase in the history of the Ulster conflict. That this phase had been delayed so long was due to two causes: the Chichester-Clark Government, with the backing of the majority of Protestant opinion, realized that, in practice, the arrival of the Army would effectively end its responsibility for the keeping of order and would transfer the control of Ulster's domestic policy, in fact though not in name, to Whitehall. Knowing that in the British Government's eyes it was already in the dock as the defender of Protestant supremacy, the Stormont Government clung desperately to such independence as it still had. Ignoring all the portents, it tried to depend solely on the police for the restoration of order.

Equally, the British Government had no taste for direct involvement in Ulster's affairs; it preferred the role of a remote critic with no immediate responsibility. It suited both parties to accept the proposition that military aid would not be invoked until local resources had been exhausted. Since the only substantial local resource which remained untapped was the B-Special Reserve of the RUC, and since that Reserve was already firmly identified in the minds of Whitehall as a sectarian paramilitary force and the very symbol of Protestant oppression, Chichester-Clark's dilemma was acute. He postponed the mobilizing of the B-Specials until it was too late for them to do anything but provide a further pretext for the view that Britain herself must now undertake the radical reform of Ulster's institutions.

That view was now carefully emphasized in everything which the British Government did. Although the reform programme, now well under way, had been initiated by Stormont, the British Government seemed bent on implying that it had been extorted by British pressure. The Stormont Government, it was implied, was under close supervision by British officials and by Mr Callaghan personally. It was, to all intents and purposes, to be treated as the agent of the British Government in carrying out a reconstruction of Northern Irish institutions. Although it retained its constitutional control of security, it was the understanding that all security forces would be under the ultimate command of the GOC and, obviously, the GOC took his orders from Whitehall. To Northern Irish Protestants, these arrangements necessarily appeared humiliating. Predictably, they produced an immediate falling-off in Unionist support for Chichester-Clark, and this meant in practice a falling-off of support for, or acceptance of, the very reforms which it was the British Government's intention to foster.

Had it been the British Government's settled intention to destroy Stormont and itself to take over the task of bringing Northern Ireland to its senses, there would be something to be said for the political actions which followed the arrival of troops in August. What is more, a blatantly and coherently anti-Stormont policy would also have had something to be said for it. The immediate reaction of the Catholic population to the arrival of the Army was favourable; the danger came from the Protestant population, although its support might well have been won by firm security policies designed to convince the majority that Britain, while dedicated to reform, would not tolerate disorder. There was already enough general dissatisfaction with what were felt to be the dithering policies of Stormont to make such a bid for general popularity on the part of the British Government feasible. Like all other coherent policies, however, this was rejected. Indeed, the only substantial addition to the reform programme which followed the arrival of the troops and the assumption of Mr Callaghan's Messianic role was one which had the inevitable consequence of weakening the Province's already inadequate provision for law-keeping.

On 21 August 1969, Lord Hunt of Mount Everest fame was appointed Chairman of a Commission (ostensibly, of course, by the Stormont Government) to report on the structure of the Royal Ulster Constabulary. By 10 October it had reported, making the recommendations which everyone knew that it would. The chief of these were that Ulster's police should, in future, cease to be armed save, like the police forces in Britain, when engaged in missions of special peril for which arms would be specifically issued; that the B-Specials (an armed Volunteer

Reserve intended, and almost exclusively used, for Border patrol and the defence of military and civil installations against armed attack) should be disbanded; and that the command structure of the RUC should be remodelled on British lines. The Hunt Commission also proposed that a new part-time force, the Ulster Defence Regiment, under military instead of police authority, should be set up to discharge the functions hitherto performed by the B-Specials.

Possibly the least of the objections to these proposals at the time they were made was the horror and consternation which they were bound to arouse even among moderate Unionists. They led immediately to rioting which caused three deaths. What in the long run was much more serious was the false prognostication on which the Report was based, about the nature of the operation in which the security forces were now engaged. In this respect, one revealing sentence deserves quotation: 'It should not be inferred from this assessment of the possible threat from terrorism that terrorist attacks are likely.' The prevailing assumption was that the threat to order in Northern Ireland arose from inter-communal rioting. The bulk of responsibility for controlling this rioting would in future rest with the Army, which would have the advantage of not being associated with either side in the traditional conflict. The police should revert as soon as possible to a civilian role, and concern themselves mainly with the suppression of ordinary crime which had no political overtones. In that task, the argument was, they would be assisted rather than impeded by being converted into a totally civilian force.

The crucial fact (which was obvious to many close observers of the Northern Irish scene) was that the conflict was now moving into a new phase, a phase which, from the start, it had been predestined to enter. The Civil Rights Movement having demonstrated that Stormont was incapable of maintaining order, and a Protestant reaction of enough ferocity having been provoked, the time was ripe for the IRA to come on to the stage. On 17 August 1969 a gelignite-laden van was driven to the door of the Crossmaglen Police Station. On the same day the IRA in Dublin officially announced that Northern units had been defending Catholic areas which had been 'attacked by deliberately fomented sectarian forces backed by the Specials with the aim of destroying the natural solidarity and unity of working-class people'.

Hitherto, the view strongly encouraged by the British Government and by moderate Unionists at Stormont had been that the IRA was not directly involved in the current batch of Ulster troubles, and that suggestions that it was so involved arose from hallucinations of the 'Reds under the bed' variety. Later, the Scarman Commission was to make much of the theory that the errors of the RUC in handling the August troubles in Belfast had arisen largely from the sincere but erroneous conviction that these troubles were the products of an IRA plot. The truth of the matter —that the IRA was content to give mild encouragement to civil disturbances, which were rapidly gathering momentum, until the right moment came for it to intervene directly—was not grasped. The riots in August—and in particular the bitter Protestant reaction in Belfast—were the signal for open IRA intervention. Throughout 1970 the pattern of violence in Ulster steadily changed. Although inter-communal violence continued on the streets, there was an increasing number of bomb attacks on public installations and private property, a large proportion of which took place in Border areas. The Army was soon driven to the expedient of spiking unapproved roads between the North and the Republic: by the spring of 1970, it was manifest that both wings of the IRA were deeply involved. The phenomenon, destined to become familiar, of public, massively attended IRA funerals, with volleys fired over the grave, had already appeared.

This meant that militarily as well as politically the conflict had changed in nature. The security forces were in future to be engaged in a guerilla war. All experience has shown that one of the indispensable conditions for success in such a war is accurately detailed intelligence. Another is the existence within the community of a body of men willing to co-operate with the authorities. Guerilla wars are not won by massive armies but by applying to the enemy the same techniques of penetration as he relies on himself. In 1969, a force specifically trained and seasoned in many campaigns of guerilla warfare against the IRA existed in Northern Ireland. The B-Special Reserve (established by Mr Lloyd George's Government in 1920 round a nucleus of volunteers which had sprung up to defend life and property against the IRA), in the eyes of most Protestants, was the principal physical guarantor of the existence of the Northern Irish State. A volunteer auxiliary force, under the control of the police and ultimately of the Northern Irish Ministry of Home Affairs, its members operated in their own immediate neighbourhoods.

They were allowed to keep their arms at home. They were expected to act as perpetual sentinels, to note the arrival of new and therefore suspicious figures in their localities, and to observe and report on anything which might portend terrorist activity. They had played a conspicuous and indeed decisive part in defeating the IRA campaign which lasted from 1957 to 1963. They checked the traffic on roads across the Border, guarded power stations and water works and were only occasionally called upon to reinforce the police in the suppression of riots. In earlier troubles, they were also often used to assist in searches.

It was hardly surprising that this force should have earned the undying hostility of those who wished to destroy the State, since it had for many years undoubtedly been the chief obstacle to their success. That the existence of such an armed force, operating in what might be described as a relatively freelance style, constituted some sort of danger to civil liberty need not be denied. The need for the B-Specials arose precisely from the fact that Northern Ireland, at the best of times, was in a state of suspended siege. Horror stories about the brutality they were alleged to have displayed on certain occasions were rife and an established part of Republican mythology, and these stories were fiercely repudiated by the force and its admirers. It is neither possible nor important here to investigate these charges. What matters is to establish the nature and function of the force. It was emphatically not a body of Protestant fanatics. It had no political motivations other than its devotion to the existence of the State. History had ensured, however, that it should be almost entirely Protestant in composition: many Catholics who had no objection to its existence did not regard it as a force to which it would be natural for them to belong. Clearly, this was a defect in its composition and one which confirmed all the suspicions of British liberals.

What mattered, however, was that in 1969 it was the one force in Northern Ireland thoroughly equipped to engage in combat with the IRA. As a source of intelligence alone it was indispensable. Inevitably, the United Kingdom Army was profoundly deficient in this respect. It was operating in a strange and largely hostile community about which it knew virtually nothing. The disbanding of the B-Specials at this juncture, therefore, was not only taken as a deep insult to the Protestant community in general, but it deprived the security forces, at the very outset of their battle with the IRA, of the most formidable weapon at their command.

The disarming and reorganizing of the RUC was open to the same sort of objection. The force felt that it had been put in the dock. Its morale, already weakened by a year's battle against impossible odds, was still further damaged by a British policeman, Sir Arthur Young, who combined a profound ignorance of the Northern Irish scene with an infallible capacity for causing offence by even the most innocent of gestures and words. As time went on, the provision that the police should be disarmed except when engaged on dangerous missions lost much importance in practice, since almost all of the missions became dangerous. For a while, however, the Army was forced to bear the heavy additional burden of providing constant protection for the disarmed police.

Many revolutions are helped by the ineptitude of government. There are few recorded instances in history, however, of a government so obliging to its assailants as the British Government was to the IRA in 1969. All was with the best intentions, but it positively co-operated in undermining respect for the agents of law and order and in depriving them of the means of defending the community. As a consequence, an ever-increasing burden of police duty fell upon the Army. Its size had to be steeply and continually increased. The British Government, however, was no more prepared for this than for any of the other inevitable consequences of its policy. General Freeland felt constrained to say that '. . . the Army may not stay long enough or may not be allowed to stay long enough, to solve the problems . . .', a threat which could carry little terror for anyone but the law-abiding majority of the population. This indiscretion was rapidly cancelled by the Prime Minister, but the Government was plainly not willing to reinforce the Army on the scale deemed necessary by Chichester-Clark.

Accordingly, on 20 March, under increasingly bitter attack from the Unionist supporters, and having failed to convince the British Government of the imperative need for a tougher security policy, Chichester-Clark resigned, in order to bring home to all concerned 'the realities of the present constitutional, political and security situation'. So passed into history another reforming Unionist Prime Minister who had striven valiantly to achieve the objectives which the British Government professed to want. Clearly, Northern Ireland was far nearer a state of civil war than it had been on his accession. Moreover, two new factors, latent from the first, had come into play—the IRA and the Dublin Government. Responding to the riots in August 1969, Mr Lynch, hitherto content with a role of benevolent neutrality towards Catholic Ulster, had made a number of gestures calculated to arouse bitter Protestant antagonism. He had established field stations on the Republican side of the Border to provide treatment for those injured in the North and afraid to fall into the hands of the authorities. He had suggested the sending of a United Nations force or an Anglo-Irish force to restore order in the North. Following riots in the summer of 1970, a large number of Catholics from Belfast, to the accompaniment of much publicity, sought 'refuge' in the South: the Dublin Government set up reception centres for them. Most of them, however, much dissatisfied with the arrangements made for their comfort, soon decided to return home to the evident relief of their Southern hosts. There was, of course, no practical possibility of military intervention by the Republic, but from henceforth the Southern Government was to assume much more explicitly than hitherto the role of guardian of Catholic Ulster, and was to demand an increasing say in the shaping of British policy towards the Province. The IRA and the Dublin Government, therefore, were two more elements for the British Government to take into account in ordering Ulster's affairs. They provided two more opportunities for comprehensive misunderstanding.

Chapter 5

The IRA

In the campaign from 1957 to 1963 the IRA had suffered a crippling defeat. As a consequence, it had been obliged to review its total role in Irish politics. Hitherto, its own view of its credentials had been clear and uncompromising. It was, so it believed, the sole legitimate heir of the Republican tradition in Ireland. The abortive declaration of an Irish Republic during the Easter Rising of 1916 had created a sovereign though abstract entity, the Irish State, which was morally entitled to the obedience of all Irishmen. The IRA was the sole surviving agent of that entity; it was in perpetual war against all who denied or encroached on the sovereign rights of the Irish people. This meant in the first instance that it was at war with Britain, and must remain so until the Parliament at Westminster abandoned its claim to ultimate authority in the Six Counties. It also meant, however, that it was at war with all representatives of lawful authority in the South, for the Southern State, whether in the form of the Irish Free State or the *soi-disant* Irish Republic, had forfeited any title to allegiance by its acceptance of the settlement of 1922 and its *de facto* recognition of the Border.

In its own eyes, therefore, the IRA was not a political movement struggling for the realization of an ideal; it was the representative and executive arm of an actual State. As such, it was called upon not only to expel foreign invaders and occupiers but also to punish Irishmen who denied its writ. Moreover, the attainment of Irish unity in itself would not satisfy the IRA's claims. The movement was wedded to the theory that the entire social and political structure of the South was of alien origin and that the *bourgeois* Republic there was capable of surviving only by virtue of its dependence on foreign capital.

The IRA's political philosophy was a somewhat indistinct compound of extreme Nationalism and Socialist centralism. Since all established political institutions in Ireland were, in its eyes, illegitimate, it declined to participate in their running by putting up candidates at elections. As it was an illegal organization in the South no less than in the North it was prepared to circumvent the law for the purpose of gaining a public forum by maintaining a political wing in the form of Sinn Fein; but the IRA did not conceive itself as being in any way dependent on this wing. Technically and in practice, its political direction was in the hands of its own army council.

After 1963, however, it became doubtful whether these rigid positions could be maintained. The campaign in the North had not only thoroughly alienated Catholic opinion there, it had also aroused intense anger in the South. *Fianna Fail*, the ruling party there, was indeed the heir to that section of the Republican movement which had rejected the treaty of 1922 and fought a bloody and bitter civil war against the Free State Government. A section of the party, as events in 1970 were dramatically to show, still had IRA sympathies, but the party as a whole wanted peace, stability and economic progress on sound *bourgeois* lines. Eamon de Valera, the greatest surviving Republican hero of the Anglo-Irish war and the Irish civil war, and Prime Minister of the Free State and the Republic for a total of twenty-one years and President from 1959 to 1973, was now the epitome of respectable elder-statesmanship.

In this hostile atmosphere, the dominant trend in the IRA was towards revisionism. It developed a Left-wing intelligentsia which preached the need for alignment with modern revolutionary movements, and urged the value of entering politics and penetrating progressive political parties, and of judiciously exploiting popular grievances. As the 'sixties progressed, the Dublin Government encountered an increasing measure of difficulty from social protest (squatting, demonstrations by farmers aggrieved at low agricultural prices, and attacks on foreign-owned property), and it was evident that much of this was inspired by the IRA. When the Civil Rights Movement appeared in the North, it immediately became an object of IRA interest and encouragement, although this was at first mixed with scepticism about the efficacy of 'passive' disobedience.

From the first, however, a hard core of IRA opinion opposed the move towards modernization. Several elements in the new thinking were profoundly distasteful to it. The Left Wing of the IRA, for instance, tended to be anti-clerical. It also gave a far higher immediate importance to social than to national protest.

56

Neither wing, it must be emphasized, repudiated violence or renounced the ultimate aim of Irish Unity. The dispute was essentially about tactics rather than strategic ends.

In December 1969 came about the split which had been impending for some time. Henceforth, there were to be two clearly distinguished and bitterly hostile IRA movements—the Official and the Provisional, with their respective political wings. Both went openly into action in the North after August 1969. The 'Provos', adhering to the old view of the IRA as the sole legitimate guardian of Irish sovereignty, claimed that its Northern brigade had provided protection for Belfast Catholics against the Protestant rabble in the great riots of August, but this was soon followed by a statement from Cathal Goulding, Commander-in-Chief of the Official IRA, to the effect that it now seemed clear that Irish unity could only be achieved by force. The two movements were fiercely hostile to each other: the casualty lists of Northern Ireland over the ensuing years included many murders of Provos by Officials, and vice versa; and countless others go unrecorded because of the lack of interest which they aroused in the security forces which were, until 1972, under equal attack from both. The principal difference between campaigns of the Officials and the Provos in the North was that on the whole Official violence was more selective. The Officials were happy to murder soldiers, policemen, capitalists and exploiting landowners, but they thought that indiscriminate bombing of civilians and attacks on the Protestant working class were counter-productive. Their social propaganda tended to be couched in the idiom of Marxism and its deviations. They spoke of a 'United Irish Working Class Republic'.

By contrast, the Provisionals were traditionalist revolutionaries. In 1970, they published a social programme demanding a United Ireland organized largely on a basis of kibbutz farming. Later on, while never abandoning their claim to embody the latent sovereignty of the Irish people, they accepted as their first objective the reconstitution of the historic Province of Ulster to consist of nine counties and to be organized on a basis of federalism and maximum devolution. The immediate aim, in the pursuit of which they remained unwavering, was a total end to Britain's political connection with Northern Ireland.

The split in the IRA had two important consequences. It led to a crucial although not generally recognized difference in emphasis in the attitudes of the British and Dublin Governments towards the two IRAS. From the first, Dublin was far more afraid of the Officials than of the Provisionals. It was the Officials who challenged most powerfully the Establishment in the South. It was the Officials who were on the alert to inflame all popular discontent with the *bourgeois* Republic. From Dublin's point of view, the Provisionals at least had the merit of operating beyond the Border. As interest in Northern Ireland increased, the social agitation mounted by the Officials in the Republic tended to decline. A substantial element in the *Fianna Fail* party, which remained in power until March 1973, kept its militant Republican sympathies and its support went naturally to the Provisionals. The danger arising from this source certainly appeared less to some moderate Dublin politicians because it inevitably relieved the pressure to which the Dublin Government was subject from Official activity in the South. The extent to which Dublin has bought its peace at the expense of Ulster must not be exaggerated, but neither must it be ignored.

The second consequence of the split cannot yet be fully measured. On 29 May 1972 the Official IRA made a truce in Ulster which has survived ever since. Like most Ulster truces it was hedged in by innumerable qualifications: it did not exclude, for instance, 'defensive action' against the Army and the police. Nevertheless, its existence has been recognized by the British and it has purchased for the Official IRA in the North a substantial immunity from arrest and detention. There is no evidence that the organization of the Officials has suffered from the military inactivity which followed the truce. A powerful and highly organized revolutionary movement, other than the Provos, remains in being. What part it may choose to play in the *dénouement* of the Ulster plot remains to be seen.

It was the Provisionals, however, who emerged as the chief enemy. It was therefore of crucial importance that the nature of that movement, the definiteness of its aims and its uncompromising commitment to them should be understood by the British. Over a period of years, the Provos, like Hitler before them, were at pains to make plain not only what they stood for but precisely how they meant to get it. From time to time, they sought in public (though not very hard) to counteract the unfavourable impression produced by these revelations, to suggest that they were striving only for constitutional liberty or the end of internment. Characteristically, it has been these casual tributes to moderation which have been most avidly seized upon in Britain.

In 1972, a leading member of the Provisional IRA had a conversation with an Englishman resident in Dublin, the contents of which were recorded verbatim. They are reproduced here as supplying one of the clearest available expositions of Provisional thinking. This orthodoxy in all its essentials remains unchanged.

Question: *National opinion in the South and a growing proportion of Catholics in Northern ghettoes want to give the British initiatives a chance to work. Why then do you insist on continuing a campaign of violence?*

Answer: We are not interested in seeking public support of any kind for our actions: we are convinced that the Declaration of 1916 gives us the right and the duty to eject the British from Ireland by whatever means we choose.

But Mr Lynch, the elected head of the Irish Government, has himself said that in the present situation the immediate withdrawal of British troops would pose a grave threat to the security and lives of the Catholic minority.

Mr Lynch does not represent the Republican Movement: on the contrary he is a willing collaborator of the British, only anxious to preserve the system created artificially by the 1921 Government of Ireland Act. He is a traitor to the cause of Irish unity.

You imply that whatever the British propose with regard to the North, you have no confidence in their good faith, notwithstanding the cautious welcome given to the latest proposals by the Irish Government?

No British Government proposals can ever be trusted, nor has any British Minister any right whatever to interfere in any part of the 32 counties. The British are imperialist and colonialist exploiters; they are implacably hostile to Ireland and they must be driven out.

But if an elected Irish Government appears to represent, in its policies towards the North, the consensus of view of most people in the South, who are you to deny the democratic rights of that majority when they seek, via Mr Lynch, a negotiated peaceful means of reuniting the country?

I repeat, the leadership of the Republican Movement is historically vested in the Provisional IRA: it is therefore irrelevant to consider the policies of collaboration followed by Mr Lynch.

But why not gain support for your attitudes—give it a firm political base— by agreeing to cease your campaign of violence for a period and thereby allow Mr Whitelaw to speed up the release of internees, if not to end internment altogether? You would thus attract enormous credit in the eyes of your co-religionists in the North and in the South.

The end of internment in the North would be the best thing for the British and the worst thing for us. If internment were ended, it would be the end for us in the North. You must remember that we were sold out in 1921: we will never allow this to happen again. That means that the struggle of the last three years must not be permitted to wither away when we are in sight of victory.

If you are not concerned with political isolation within the Republican Movement—even the Official IRA reject your tactics—how do you propose to achieve unity of Ireland supposing that the sectarian violence you are embarked upon results in civil war and a situation where the British depart?

If the first part of your question refers to the Official IRA let us get one thing clear. The Officials have no mandate to represent Republicanism: they are in open alliance with Communists in 'front' organizations and they have explicitly recognized the legitimacy of the Free State *Dail*. As to what we would do when we have driven the British out of Ireland, you can leave that to be settled between Irishmen.

But there are over a million Irishmen, not all of the Protestant faith, in the North, who have rejected—at least for the time being—the concept of a united Ireland. What is your answer to them?

If Irishmen prove traitors to the cause of a united Ireland then they must get out of the country with their British friends. The majority of the Irish people want a united Ireland, and it is their will which must prevail. Ours is not a sectarian struggle—that is a lie put out by the British—and what I have said about traitors applies as much to Catholics as to Protestants.

Even to what seems to be large numbers of Catholics in the South?

Certainly. The people in the 26 counties have been misled and betrayed by their so-called leaders for years. We stand for a united 32 county Ireland, not for rule by *Fianna Fail* and the Free Staters. It is a system which has only existed for so long because the Special Branch, instead of protecting Irish interests, has been used to attack the Republican Movement and to collaborate openly with the British occupiers.

You imply that you wish to destroy the system of government in the South and to impose on a perhaps unwilling population your own version of Republican rule.

That is the greatest and most difficult task ahead of us. Centralized Government in Dublin, as represented by *Fianna Fail* and *Fine Gael,* is corrupt: the spoils of power and patronage go, as they always have, to a group of businessmen and politicians who have no interest whatever in the well-being of Irishmen. They pay lip service to the revival of the first official language and literally starve Irishmen out of the western areas. We advocate, as you know, a system of regional government which will give full weight to local interests and break the monopoly of the Dublin politicians.

But are you not as likely to provoke civil war in the South by a programme of action—as in the North—which has not been endorsed by the majority of the population?

That is a typical distortion, if I may say so. Once the people see that the Republican Movement is determined to achieve its aims, only those who reject national unity will identify themselves as the enemies of Ireland. Irish independence was born in the blood of patriots in 1916; so it will be again.

Chapter 6

Illusions about Dublin

The failure of Britain to understand the nature of the IRA is paralleled by her failure to grasp the part which Southern Ireland as a whole has been playing in the Ulster conflict. From 1968 onwards, the Irish Republic has provided a more or less secure place for the planning of IRA action in the North and a more or less safe haven for IRA refugees from Northern justice. The alterations between the 'more' and the 'less' have depended upon the vicissitudes of Southern Irish politics. Today (March 1975), the Republic is beyond doubt less hospitable to the IRA than it ever was during the whole of this period. Its courts, however, still regularly refuse to extradite even the most dangerous criminals if they can establish that their crimes were politically motivated. Six years after the beginning of the conflict, an attempt to provide a substitute for extradition, in the shape of a law authorizing Southern Irish courts to try offences alleged to have been committed in Ulster or Britain by criminals who had taken refuge in the Republic, is still fighting its way to the Statute Book against the most vigorous opposition. Internment, frequently and successfully used by the Republic in the past, and threatened as recently as 1970 by Mr Lynch, has not been employed at all in the South during the current troubles. A substitute for it—the establishment of special courts operating without juries to try offences against the State by rules of evidence designed to favour the prosecution—was not provided until December 1972. Before this, prosecutions which might have political repercussions were frequently avoided. In November 1971, for example, it was estimated that the Republic had suffered in the last four and a half years nineteen raids on banks, post offices and airline offices involving a total loss of £100,000, most of which was believed to have gone into the pockets of the IRA. Only five of these cases had got as far as prosecution and no one had at the time been convicted for these offences. Under the constitution of the Irish Republic there is no Public Prosecutor, and prosecutions for political offences are accordingly initiated by the Attorney General who is, of course, a member of the Government. This, it is constantly complained, introduces a political element into the decision about what charges should be pressed. Sometimes, when a prosecution for an IRA offence was brought, a lesser charge would be substituted for a more serious one. A flagrant instance of this was the case of four men in November 1971 who were believed to have fired across the Border at British troops. They were given a fortnight's imprisonment for possessing firearms and ammunition without certificates. In Border areas where the IRA had strong popular support, juries would often refuse to convict. A Londonderry man accepted full responsibility for two hand grenades found in his possession when charged at Donegal Court in July 1971. He was cleared by a jury and the Court applauded. Judge Ryan commented: 'I'm glad, gentlemen, that that's your verdict, not mine.' Even now, the only charge easily available for use in the South against an IRA man from the North is that of membership of an illegal organization, and this commonly carries with it only a few months' imprisonment.

Public collections for IRA funds in the Republic (in spite of the fact that the organization is illegal) were a familiar feature of life until the end of 1972. At no time has the gentle and intermittent harassment of the IRA by the Government in Dublin impeded the ready access to IRA leaders of British journalists and television interviewers. Among the factors which made the IRA campaign in the North possible—lavish financial support from deluded Irish Americans, and guns and technical advice from Iron Curtain and Middle and Far Eastern Countries—the acquiescence of the Republic in IRA activity has almost certainly been the most powerful. To put it in the mildest possible terms, the Republic has not prevented a war against a neighbouring friendly power from being waged from the Republic's territory. In 1970, Mr Lynch suddenly dismissed two senior ministers, Mr Haughey and Mr Blaney, for alleged conspiracy in gun-running in the North. Subsequently there were abortive prosecutions and investigations. All that emerged was that both armaments and public money had reached the IRA with more or less high level connivance in the Republic. British opinion was momentarily scandalized, but the incident was rapidly dismissed as another example of the eccentricity of Irish politics.

What has to be explained, then, is why the British Government and the British people, while ready to spend lives and money year after year on the task of restoring order in the North, had been prepared to acquiesce in the pusillanimity towards the IRA shown by Dublin. 'Aquiesce' is not too strong a word. Indeed, Dublin has been positively rewarded for its part in these affairs by an ever-growing degree of consultation with Whitehall about Northern Ireland policy. Mr Lynch's gestures of support towards Catholic Ulster, and his invocations of the United Nations after the riots in August 1969, elicited the traditional and correct British response: Sir Alec Douglas-Home reminded Dr Hillery, the Republic Foreign Minister, that Northern Ireland was part of the United Kingdom and as such a domestic concern of the British Government. As late as August 1971, an injudicious telegram of exhortation, sent by Mr Lynch to Mr Heath in the course of a top-level meeting between the British and Northern Irish Governments at Chequers, evoked an extremely sharp retort from the British Prime Minister. However, reconciliation followed shortly after, and Mr Lynch was soon himself being entertained at Chequers. From then on periodic meetings between the British and Southern Irish Prime Ministers (in which occasionally Mr Faulkner and his senior colleagues from the North were invited to participate) became the rule until, in December 1973, the climax was reached in the Sunningdale Conference. This, by going to the furthest point yet reached in acceptance of the Republic's demands, effectively ensured the failure of the Northern Irish Executive and left Britain's Northern Irish policy in ruins.

The explanation of this seemingly inexhaustible patience with Dublin relates once more to one of the main themes of this analysis—the obsession of British politicians with the idea of 'the centre'. Just as in Ulster Britain strove constantly to create a political centre, so she was convinced that in the Republic the centre, in the shape of Mr Lynch and his moderate colleagues in *Fianna Fail*, was already in charge and must at all costs be kept so. Mr Lynch, it was known, had only a minute majority in the *Dail* (the Southern Irish Parliament), and British observers did not always realize that this was neither a very remarkable phenomenon under an electoral system based on proportional representation, nor a very serious source of weakness to a political party which lived under an almost military discipline and had acquired over decades of power an outstanding skill in the manipulation of patronage. In fact, Mr Lynch was seldom in the degree of political danger which British politicians suspected. What is more remarkable, however, is the failure of the British to realize that the consequence of the defeat of the Lynch Administration at any time would have been almost wholly favourable to the interests of British policy. *Fianna Fail*, though most of it had become *bourgeois* and respectable, had, in theory, inherited the mantle of militant republicanism. Historically, it was the anti-partition party. What is more, as popular reaction to the alleged arms smuggling affair showed, it had a lunatic fringe which was thoroughly behind the IRA, and this fringe had considerable popular support in Border areas like Donegal. Had Mr Lynch been beaten in the *Dail*, however, the result would have been a General Election which would have returned not the gun-runners but the *Fine Gael* to power.

Historically, this was the Free State party and it was now pre-eminently the party of law and order. The failure of the Lynch Government to clamp down promptly and effectively on the IRA arose partly from fear of alienating *Fianna Fail*'s extreme Republican wing, and partly—as the opposition frequently urged—from the sheer inefficiency bred of a long period of political supremacy during which, according to well-established Irish custom, public offices, including even judicial offices, had been freely distributed as political rewards. To have this mess cleared up by an efficient political party under Liam Cosgrave, whose father had been the terror of the IRA in the 'twenties, could only have served the purposes of Britain. The British Government, however (powerfully assisted, one suspects, by its diplomatic advisers in Dublin), seemed to have reached the conclusion that the preservation of Lynch was a primary British interest. When, in March 1973, Lynch went to the country, it was noticeable that British observers in Dublin greeted his defeat and the election of the Cosgrave *Fine Gael*-Labour Coalition with extreme anxiety. A curious defence for this strange reaction was fashionable at the time. It used to be sagely remarked by those in the confidence of the British Government that Cosgrave might well be a tougher, more realistic and more anti-IRA Prime Minister than Lynch, but that, driven into Opposition, *Fianna Fail* would fall into the hands of the wild men in its ranks. This would mean that the 'alternative Government' in the Republic would be blatantly in favour of the IRA. This preference for having a bad party in power rather than risking making it worse by driving it into Opposition is a striking example of the lengths to which casuistry can go.

Underlying this astonishing misreading of the politics of the Republic was a huge error about the feelings of the people of the South towards the Ulster crisis. The British saw Lynch, a wise and moderate man, controlling, by a rare combination of guile and firmness, what they believed to be a mass public demand in the Republic for positive aid to the oppressed Catholics of Ulster; but nothing could have been further from the truth. Outside a limited circle of Republican sympathizers in Dublin and a few traditionally militant areas like Donegal, there was an overwhelming apathy about the whole Northern question. Matters such as the wisdom of joining the Common Market, and the progress of inflation, absorbed most people's attention for most of the time, a fact dramatically illustrated by the election campaign of 1973. In so far as the North was even considered, it was largely as one aspect of the law and order question in the South. Emotive events like 'Bloody Sunday' in 1972 inevitably stirred a public reaction, although the burning of the British Embassy in Dublin on that occasion was largely a deliberately contrived demonstration by the IRA. What is more, almost everybody from Southern Ireland will affirm as a matter of theology that he believes in Irish Unity. For long, however, this aspiration has been a part of folklore to be celebrated on convivial occasions in song and verse. When it comes to action, however, the idea of intervention in the North fills the average Southerner with consternation. Not only is such a thing physically impossible because of the military weakness of the Republic, but the success of the enterprise, if it were conceivable, would spell the doom of the Irish Republic.

The Republic is constructed to express the ethnic and cultural identity of a Gaelic, Catholic, largely rural community. This ideological basis is largely fraudulent, but it remains the foundation of the State. Although in December 1972 the Republic resolved by referendum to remove from its constitution the special recognition of the Roman Catholic Church, there is in fact little enthusiasm for any of the other changes (the abolition, for example, of the clause which makes the legalization of divorce unconstitutional) which are recommended as means of preparing the way for unification. Naturally enough, the feeling is that there is something absurd in inviting the South to abandon all its distinctive institutions simply in order to vindicate the

66

proposition that its people are part of an Irish nation which transcends the Border.

But apart from these deep considerations, the factors which make unification a distasteful, not to say a horrifying, prospect for any Southern Irishmen who soberly consider it, are innumerable. The idea of acquiring a turbulent Protestant working class traditionally given to sectarian rioting has no appeal at all. The idea of absorbing the militant Northern Republicans— more aggressive on the whole than their Southern counterparts —is positively terrifying. The burden on the Southern Irish economy which would be imposed by adding to the depressed areas of the South those of the North, and transferring to the Dublin Exchequer the cost of Northern welfare now borne by Britain, would be intolerable.

None of this, however, alters the fact that tradition requires all Southern Irish politicans to subscribe to the idea of Irish unity. That is particularly so in the case of *Fianna Fail*, but it is also true of *Fine Gael*. The Free Staters accepted the settlement of 1922 because it was the best compromise available, and they have always denied vigorously the charge that in so doing they renounced the ideal of Irish unity. They also, therefore, are required to make public obeisance to this ideal. What would have suited the governments both of Mr Lynch and of Mr Cosgrave best would have been a swift return to order in the North on the basis of some sort of settlement which could have been represented as a step in the direction of Catholic emancipation and, if possible, Irish unity. On the face of it, there was no compelling reason why the British Government should meet even those requirements. Britain would appear to have irresistible means of putting pressure on the South, and these, one might have supposed, would have dispensed with the need for offering concessions. A ban on Irish immigration into Britain, for example, would cripple the economy of the Republic. A 'trade war' would be equally fatal to the prosperity of the South and inflict relatively little discomfort on Britain. The failure of Dublin Governments to prevent the use of their territory as a base for hostile operations against the United Kingdom would have provided full juridical justification for such measures.

Plainly, however, these suggestions belong to the realms of fantasy. Open coercion of this kind would undoubtedly have aroused a strong Nationalist reaction in the South. At the best, these threats would have to be kept in the background and carried out only *in extremis*. The mystery was, however, that Britain behaved towards the Republic as though it were she rather than the Republic who was the dependent partner. When it came to offering concessions in order to persuade Dublin to offer at least minimal co-operation in defeating the IRA, there were only two which Britain could make without appearing to violate her obligations to Ulster.

First, she could give *de facto* recognition to the special interest of the Republic in Northern affairs by consulting the Republic when shaping Northern Irish policy. From the Republic's point of view this would be an immense advance on the past, for the view that Ulster was an exclusively United Kingdom concern had always been jealously guarded. In addition to this, Britain could give formal recognition not to the unity of Ireland as an ideal, but to the right of the people of the North to opt, should they ever wish to, for union with the South. Even these concessions would carry the gravest dangers and could be exposed to very serious moral objections. Is regular consultation with Dublin fully consistent with Northern Ireland's status as part of the United Kingdom? Suppose a bare majority of the people of Northern Ireland were one day to choose unification while a substantial minority, largely concentrated in one part of the territory, were to remain bitterly opposed to it? Would it be morally justifiable to hand that minority over, or would a strict regard for self-determination rather enjoin the redrawing of the frontier? On balance, Britain and the Protestant North might well think that consultation, plus an understanding to accept unification at some distant future date should unification be desired by the majority in Northern Ireland, represented a price worth paying for the invaluable asset of immediate Southern support against the IRA.

In the event, however, both these priceless concessions were simply dished out to Dublin without the exaction of any tangible return. Consultation with the Republic became a regular habit, and at Sunningdale the principle of self-determination was conceded in the clearest possible terms. Although Mr Cosgrave's Government has been predictably tougher than Mr Lynch's in its handling of the IRA, extradition, or an effective substitute for it, is still awaited.

The British Government had the most favourable imaginable conditions for a successful bargain with Dublin. Through its almost incredible failure to understand Southern Irish politics it failed to bargain at all. Instead, it made a series of gestures to the South which bore fruit only in Protestant suspicion and hostility in the North, and which thereby contributed directly to the wrecking of its policy.

Chapter 7

Faulkner: Mark I

Of the failures of British statesmen in their handling of Ulster since 1969, few have been more remarkable and more disastrous in their consequences than their failure to understand the character of Brian Faulkner and the strength and limitations of his position in the Province's policies. Here was a man who, to an extent far greater than O'Neill or Chichester-Clark, had it in his power to 'deliver' the Ulster Unionist party, and with it the great majority of Protestants, into the British Government's camp, provided that the conditions imposed upon him were not such as to make their acceptance seem like an act of betrayal. Here also was a man whose political philosophy consisted almost entirely of one principle—the principle that Ulster's survival depended on the preservation of the Union and that almost any price was worth paying to secure that end. Here, above all, was a man with a natural bent towards compromise.

This, however, was not the picture of Faulkner which had established itself in the minds of the British Government and the British people. To them, he was an unimaginative hardliner, devious when it suited his personal ambition but fundamentally committed to the preservation at all costs of Protestant supremacy. Many considered him to be a quiet fanatic. Few doubted that, given half a chance, he would scrap the reform programme, remobilize the B-Specials and embark upon open conflict with Britain if ever the moment for such an adventure should seem propitious.

This fantastically false estimate was in part attributable to the fact that Brian Faulkner is so distinctively a local phenomenon, not easily to be fitted into any of the social categories with which the British are familiar. Faulkner represents something extinct in Britain—an aristocracy of trade. Three centuries of wealth and influence, based on textile manufacture and interrupted only briefly by one family disaster, have left its *bourgeois* quality totally unimpaired. It is ashamed of nothing in its ancestry but a Marchioness's daughter who behaved badly in Bath. Its culture is Presbyterian, its politics Whig. It represents *par excellence* those elements in Ulster which, though profoundly suspicious of change, have the merchants' distaste for violence and distrust of all forms of political romanticism. Faulkner was trained as a business man, and it was essentially as a business man that he approached the task of governing Ulster. Having not been permitted by his father to join up during the war, he could not ever prefix a military title to his name—something of a disadvantage in Ulster politics but a feature which once again emphasized the thoroughly civilian character of his approach.

By the time he succeeded Chichester-Clark as Prime Minister in March 1971, he had built up a considerable heritage of distrust. Ulstermen, of course, express their views in colourful and often extravagant terms. To the great political families of the old Protestant ascendancy he was 'a scheming *parvenu*'; to the thin but strident ranks of Ulster liberalism he was a reactionary who could never see when he had been beaten; to the Orange populists, the disciples of Craig and Paisley, he was 'the middle-class businessman who was trained only to sell and who would not stop short of selling Ulster'; to all the various brands of Republicanism he was 'the one man with whom we can never do business'.

Yet in March 1971, the effect of all these extreme charges was more than offset by one overwhelming asset—Faulkner's reputation for a degree of political skill comparable with that of front-rank British politicians, whose capacities still tend in Ulster to be exaggerated. Added to this was a reputation for success. His opposition to O'Neill had convinced all but extreme Unionists that he was still deploying these talents in the best interests of the Province. A concession made by Faulkner, it was still thought, must spring from some deep calculation; anyone who struck a bargain with Faulkner, it was believed, must get the worst of it. The British Government which (as Ulstermen saw it) had so far only had to deal with a dilettante (O'Neill) and an honest country gentleman of limited shrewdness (Chichester-Clark), would now have to get into the habit of counting its spoons.

In reality, Faulkner's negotiating skill, like his deviousness and lack of warmth and imagination, was much exaggerated. He is, in fact, an imaginative political schemer and a persuasive speaker. He can conceive policies and, if they are at all saleable,

71

he is adept at selling them. As a negotiator, by contrast, he is too impatient of delay and too anxious to settle to be really formidable. By giving Faulkner a few tokens of success from time to time, the British Government could have kept in the Unionists' saddle a man who was willing to go to almost any lengths to preserve the British connection. Strangely, that Government thought that its real interests lay in teaching Faulkner a lesson. In the process it shattered his support, a catastrophe to which he himself in the end contributed by his over-zealous acceptance of British leadership, and by his lack of concern (arising in part from a shy and lonely nature) with the importance of keeping his relations with Unionist colleagues in good repair.

At the beginning of his first ministry, however, Faulkner's political position was still secure. The state of play had been sharply and tragically clarified in 1970. The IRA was now engaged in open war and it was its guerilla campaign rather than continuing communal violence which, by the mid-summer of 1971, was the chief preoccupation of the security forces. The constitutional opposition to the Unionist Government had also consolidated itself. The old Nationalist party, whose doom had been sealed by the 1969 General Election, had been succeeded in the role of political spokesman for the Catholic community by the Social Democratic and Labour party. This was an amalgam of former Nationalists, Republican Labour men and independents with Civil Rights leanings. It had a social and economic programme well to the Left of the centre, but it made Irish unification still one of its primary aims. With the Civil Rights Movement now in disarray (its surviving members were to all intents and purposes now the agents of one or other branch of the IRA charged with mounting civil disorder as and when this suited the IRA), the SDLP was increasingly seen by British liberals as one of the main ingredients in that 'centre' for which British policy was searching.

As for the SDLP itself, it came under steadily growing pressure from the IRA and the Republican Movement generally. Its members were exposed to direct personal intimidation; Republicans taunted it with ineffectualness, claiming that all experience showed that the British could be bombed into submission more easily than they could be cajoled into concession. The SDLP, however, was itself (a fact never appreciated in Britain) doctrinally committed to Irish unification. Its aim now was to prove to Catholics that it could achieve more for them by diplomacy than Republicans could achieve by force. At the same time, it was bent on convincing the British Government that concession to the SDLP was the only available means of swinging Catholic opinion against terrorism. Inevitably, all this imposed an ambivalent role on the party: it could deplore violence but it could not appear to side with the security forces. Manifestly, it was violence which had lent importance to the SDLP—a newly formed minority party which had never yet been exposed to the electorate but which might hope to advance its fortunes by persuading the British that it held the key to peace in Ulster.

The party's leader and deputy leader—Mr Gerry Fitt and Mr John Hume—admirably complemented each other's qualities. Mr Fitt is an amiable and convivial man with the gift of the gab. By 1971, he had already won powerful friends at Westminster (where he sat for West Belfast) including some on the Tory front benches. He was playing a conspicuous part in shaping the Tory Government's view of Ulster, and he was listened to with far more respect than was accorded to most Ulster Unionist MPs. He had a knack of appearing flexible even when defending rigid positions, and this contrasted with Mr Faulkner's gift for appearing rigid even when falling over backwards to make concessions. Mr Hume, on the other hand, is a man of more austere character. Trained for the Church, a philanthropist who had generously spent the proceeds of his smoked salmon business in Londonderry on social and political work, a man not easily capable either of compromise or the semblance of it, he had risen to fame as a champion of civil rights. In their different ways these two men, by the middle of 1971, were manifestly working for one end—the abolition of Stormont. For different reasons, that was also the immediate objective of the IRA, but the SDLP was bent on getting there first.

In 1970, another ingredient in what the British regarded as the potential Northern Irish centre had also appeared. The Alliance party was an attempt to gather together under one roof Protestants and Catholics who, while committed to the preservation of the Union, were generally inclined to reformist policies. Its founder pointed out that the Unionist party, although it had never raised any constitutional barrier to the admission of Catholics, and although, undoubtedly, it had won many Catholic votes at general elections, was, to all intents and purposes, a Protestant party. Only rarely in its history had it been able to boast a Catholic constituency officer. Its character was further emphasized by its constitutional links with the Orange Lodges. A new party, which was ostentatiously non-sectarian in composition and which was thoroughly committed to liberal policies but at the same time bore none of the taint of Republicanism, could, it was contended, have a crucial part to play in Northern Ireland's future. Later on, the Alliance party was to win over from Mr Faulkner's allegiance a few talented members of his Left wing. It was also to play some part in encouraging him, in an effort to prevent such desertions, to adopt policies which alienated vast numbers of Right-wing Unionists, driving them into the camps of Paisley or Craig. In 1971, however, the main function of the Alliance party was to deepen British misunderstanding of Northern Ireland. Its leaders, Mr Oliver Napier (a Catholic) and Mr Bob Cooper (a Protestant), both used language thoroughly comprehensible to visiting British politicians. Their moderation, their concern for social and economic questions, their immunity from the influence of the local folklore, made them look like the answer to the British Government's prayer. These qualities, however, also ensured that their support would be almost entirely confined to a small, sophisticated section of the professional middle class. The extravagant hopes reposed in them by many British politicians helped to obscure the truth that the real centre in Ulster politics was much more nearly represented by the Unionist party, and would continue to be so represented until that party finally fell under the control of its Right wing.

For the present, however, Mr Faulkner could afford to ignore the embryonic Alliance party. The main aim of his political strategy was to disarm the SDLP by concessions which removed the last rational objection to full support for the constitution, and to effective support for the security forces in their efforts to defend the law. This was not an easy task. Already, by the end of Chichester-Clark's Administration, all the original demands of the Civil Rights Movement had been accepted and were being rapidly translated into action. Significantly, however, the SDLP had added a new demand to the list. It was not enough that the Catholic minority should be given the fullest possible legal protection in the exercise of the ordinary rights of citizenship, it must be assured of permanent representation in executive government. The argument ran thus: politics in Northern Ireland were effectively conducted on sectarian lines. This meant that the Catholic third of the population would automatically be denied representation in government. The only way of avoiding a permanent system of one-party rule in the Province would be to give political representatives of the minority a constitutional right to some share in office. To this the Unionist reply was that the exclusion of Catholic politicians from office was not an instance of sectarian prejudice but a consequence of the fact that those politicians were traditionally committed to the abolition of the Union and the achievement of a united Ireland. It was this opposition to the very existence of the State which ensured that Catholic parties would never have a share in government. If the State were accepted, a party system which reflected social and economic interests and views, rather than the perennial debate about the Border, could easily come into being. In the meantime, it was not easy to see how Catholic politicians (which meant in practice Republican politicians) could be admitted to office as of right without denying the principle of majority rule, destroying the system of collective Cabinet responsibility and, for good measure, endangering the security of the State.

This dilemma, however, did not defeat Mr Faulkner. In the early summer of 1971, he took the SDLP by surprise with a revolutionary proposal for the establishment of a new committee system at Stormont. There would be four committees with salaried chairmen, and two of these chairmanships would be reserved for Opposition members. The committees would not only be charged with the detailed examination of Government Bills and with the general duty of interrogating the Executive, they would actually have a share in the preparation of Government Bills. Although individual Cabinet Ministers would remain responsible for their Departments, these committees would have a substantial part in the running of executive government, a degree of influence, for instance, vastly greater than it has ever been seriously contemplated giving to the Opposition at Westminster. This concession may be seen in retrospect (as it appeared to many at the time) as representing the ultimate point to which a Unionist government could go in offering what was later to be known as 'power-sharing' without sealing its own doom.

Even the SDLP was hard put to it to find a decent reason for spurning this olive branch. To accept it, however, would have been to accept Stormont. It would also have been to accept a settlement which, although it vastly enhanced the rights of the minority, involved no advance at all towards the unification of

Ireland, which was still one of the party's primary aims. There is evidence that at this time Republican pressure on the SDLP greatly intensified. A genuine alliance of the constitutional Opposition with the Unionist party would have been a bitter blow for the IRA. On the other hand, a blunt rejection of Mr Faulkner's proposal would not have helped to confirm the SDLP's image in Britain as a party of moderation, genuinely opposed to violence and driven to adopt rigid postures only by the obduracy of the Unionists. In the nick of time, an untoward event came to the SDLP's rescue.

In the course of a three-day riot in Londonderry in July, two civilians were shot dead by the Army. Inevitably, there was an immediate uproar: the Army contended that one of the men was armed and the other about to throw a petrol bomb; Republican bystanders swore that both were the victims of unprovoked murder. The Ministry of Defence, after the customary inquiries, declared itself wholly satisfied with the Army's explanation. The SDLP, however, demanded an independent inquiry and Miss Bernadette Devlin set up her own private inquiry. Arguing, no doubt, that it would be disastrous if a precedent were set for an independent inquiry into the death of everyone killed by the Army in the course of what now seemed to be something like a full-scale civil war, the British Government stood firm. The SDLP instantly announced its decision to withdraw from Stormont altogether, and set up its own 'alternative assembly', an institution which rapidly faded into the background but was kept in being as a standing symbol of the SDLP's rejection of the constitution as it stood.

This affair was a turning-point in the destinies of Ulster. The responsibility for the killing of the two Londonderry civilians rested not with the Stormont Government but with the United Kingdom Army and, in the last resort, with the British Government. It was not in the power of Stormont to grant or deny the SDLP's demand for an inquiry. At the very least, withdrawal from Stormont was therefore a gesture wholly irrelevant to the affair. That withdrawal becomes intelligible only when it is recalled that the alternative to it seemed to be acceptance of a reform programme which would remove the last of the SDLP's credibly legitimate grievances. It would have been highly damaging simply to turn down the Faulkner proposals; to withdraw in protest against army brutality, on the other hand, would have a strong appeal to the liberal conscience in Britain.

76

Any lingering doubts about the praiseworthiness of the SDLP's motives on this occasion were rapidly removed by a particularly neat exercise in the rewriting of history to which many slipshod British journalists made their no doubt unwitting contribution. It soon became the practice to say that the SDLP had withdrawn from Stormont in protest against the reintroduction of internment without trial. This did not happen until 9 August; the SDLP withdrew in July, and it was from that time that it assumed its role as an extra-constitutional Opposition, confining its parliamentary activity to the drawing of its salaries and actively sponsoring passive disobedience in the shape of a rent-and-rates strike (to be maintained until after it had been admitted to office in 1973).

Mr Faulkner's political strategy had therefore been frustrated. As the summer progressed, however, political manœuvres were rapidly fading into insignificance by comparison with the growing ferocity of the war. Rioting continued sporadically, but there was a steady increase in bombing, and it became apparent that the IRA had launched a full-scale guerilla war against the civilian population of Ulster. Policing of Catholic areas, which had been weak and intermittent since the August troubles, was not adequate to the task of stemming this tide of terrorism. Witnesses, intimidated by the IRA, would not give evidence; juries exposed themselves to danger by convicting. The reorganization of the RUC and the abolition of the B-Specials had helped to dry up the best available sources of intelligence. There was no doubt either that the IRA could rely on a measure of popular Catholic support which did not arise solely from intimidation. Many Catholics, in normal times happily acquiescent in the Union, kept a residual community loyalty which prevented them from actually handing known terrorists over to the British. The complexity of the minority's feelings in this matter has never been properly understood in Britain. Strong and genuine revulsion from violence is perfectly compatible with the harbouring of violent men, partly from fear and partly from the loyalties born of kinship. The British have never grasped that effective military action in Ulster against the IRA will automatically produce a more or less hostile Catholic reaction which no amount of reform will succeed in disarming. The alternative to effective military action on the other hand, is acquiescence in the growing power of the IRA which, by virtue of intimidation and of the prestige which attends success, is equally bound to confirm the hostility of the Catholic population towards the security forces. Military success against the IRA, although it can only be achieved by methods (such as the searching of civilian property) which are bound to arouse bitter opposition for the time being, has been repeatedly shown to bear fruit in the end in better relations between the Catholic community and the Army. Generally speaking, the British Government has consistently shrunk from the unpleasant truth that temporary Catholic civilian hostility is part of the price which has to be paid for victory in Ulster. In the summer of 1971, however, it seemed that the intensification of violence and the failure of all political initiative had for once succeeded in imparting this lesson.

From the beginning of the year, several Unionists, including some of undoubted moderation, had pressed for the reintroduction of internment without trial. In British eyes the use of this weapon in peacetime was a horrifying last resort; in the eyes of the majority of Ulstermen, not to bring it into use when the Province was under the severest attack it had suffered since the 'twenties was an act of inexplicable folly. The power of administrative arrest in the interests of security had always been regarded in Ulster as an indispensable condition of the State's survival. It remained on the Statute Book, although (with one momentary exception in 1969) it had not been used since the early 'sixties. The exception in 1969 was the arrest of twenty-four suspects who were held only for forty-eight hours' interrogation. Even this had led to a considerable furore, and it was soon made clear that the British Government (whose consent to the reintroduction of internment would in practice be necessary) was in no mood to contemplate any such move. In the 'twenties, 'thirties, 'forties and 'fifties it had been accepted that the recurrent use of internment was necessary to public order. Suspected IRA men were imprisoned without trial, normally for relatively short periods. In the Irish Republic, internment was continually used during the same period, and its absolute necessity as a protection against the IRA had come to be admitted by *Fianna Fail* no less than *Fine Gael*. As late as 1970, Mr Lynch was hinting that he might be obliged to bring it back into use. The notion that Ireland can be governed without the power of administrative detention, to be employed as and when threats to the State arise, is an extremely novel one. It was paradoxical, therefore, that internment should continue to be regarded by the British Government as an 'unthinkable' device in the conditions of open war which existed in 1971. Quite apart from the special role which internment has played in Ireland, it is a weapon to which civilized states normally have recourse when threatened with civil war.

In a country where terrorist intimidation, plus a degree of sympathy with the terrorists, makes the arrest and conviction of terrorist criminals an extremely hazardous, and therefore generally impossible operation, some substitute must be found for the normal procedures of criminal justice. Internment is also an invaluable means of increasing intelligence by interrogation. It is even sometimes useful as a method of providing temporarily for the safety of informers. It acts as a deterrent to potential terrorists, as well as a means of neutralizing actual terrorists.

None of these arguments, however, found many willing ears in Whitehall or Westminster. Mr Maudling (who, as Home Secretary, was then responsible for Ulster affairs) took refuge in the formula, to which Mr Faulkner also dutifully subscribed, that it would be wrong to reintroduce internment until the Army and the police had specifically recommended it, and that no such recommendation had yet been forthcoming. In Ulster, military men were inclined to take refuge in the proposition that they were required to conduct a military operation within a general framework laid down by their political superiors in Britain, and that the kind of operation which had been designed for them was inconsistent with the use of internment save as a last resort. By early August, however, this condition seemed to have been met.

The immediate consequences of this dramatic decision were violent and predictable. There was a series of riots; bombing continued for a while at the same appalling level it had reached in July; and there were a few open gun battles between soldiers and the IRA. It was confidently announced by the SDLP and the Dublin Government that the entire Catholic population had been alienated. The end of internment was declared by the SDLP to be a *sine qua non* of further discussions with the British Government, and the party was not dislodged from this position for the better part of a year. The IRA made full use of this reaction. A number of societies dedicated to the ending of internment were set up and funds were raised to support the campaign and assist the victims of 'fascist brutality'. The demand for the end of imprisonment without trial was an invaluable propaganda cry and one which facilitated the use of 'front organizations' of a seemingly liberal character for the support of the IRA's campaign. The Labour party in Britain, although it successfully resisted the pressure of its Irish wing in favour of outright opposition to internment, was somewhat restrained and ambivalent in its support for the Tory Government's decision.

This is a convenient moment for a review of the part which internment has played in the conflict to date. It arose from a steady and dramatic intensification of violence, to which the security forces had manifestly failed to provide an answer. It was introduced with the utmost reluctance, and after prolonged delay. Largely as a result of this, the operation was managed in a somewhat hamhanded way. The authorities naturally cast their net wide over the whole Republican movement. A few relatively innocent student protesters and pamphleteers were hauled in with known terrorists. All those arrested came from the minority, a fact to be explained by the absence to date of any organized and easily identifiable Protestant terrorist movement. Nevertheless, there would have been some justification for roping in a handful of Protestant militants, and this would have made it a degree harder to condemn internment as a sectarian act.

A small batch of suspected terrorists was selected, at the outset of the operation, for deep interrogation by the police, under conditions provided by the Army, and this was productive of innumerable horror stories of which the most familiar related to detainees being obliged to walk barefoot over broken glass and being threatened with ejection from helicopters. In March 1972, the whole question of deep interrogation was examined in a report by a Committee under Lord Parker. The Commission found that the methods of deep interrogation could in some cases involve violations of the law; that in general the duress to which those under interrogation had been subjected did not amount to deliberate brutality; that United Kingdom soldiers, in the course of their training, were themselves subject to practice interrogations conducted with much the same degree of rigour. Most important of all, however, the Committee concluded that the use of these methods had, within a few weeks, yielded more information to the security forces than could otherwise have been achieved in years, and that this information had given the Army an advantage which could well prove decisive in its battle against the IRA. In spite of this, Lord Gardiner, in a minority report, advised the Government to discontinue the use of deep interrogation, and it was his advice which the Government chose to adopt. A weapon acknowledged to be of immense value was thereby discarded, but not until the fruits of its brief use had brought about a marked improvement in security.

In September 1972, after an abortive attempt to 'phase out' internment the year before, another Commission under Lord Diplock was appointed to investigate the whole system. This Commission came to the conclusion that the retention of internment (henceforth to be described as detention) in some form or other was indispensable to the success of security operations. It proposed, nevertheless, a number of changes in the system. Internment as applied by Mr Faulkner's Government was a straightforward administrative act. The authorities were empowered to detain, for the purpose of conducting preliminary investigations, after which a detention order lasting for a month could be imposed. This in turn could be converted, at the discretion of the Minister for Home Affairs, into an internment order to last at his pleasure. The Minister was assisted in considering appeals and in estimating the evidence offered by the security authorities in calling for detention or internment by an Advisory Committee, but the decision remained in his hands.

On the advice of the Diplock Commission, the British Government substituted for this purely administrative procedure a complex, semi-judicial procedure. In accordance with this, the Secretary of State was empowered to make Interim Custody Orders, which must, in the course of six weeks, be referred to a legal Commissioner who had the responsibility for confirming or ending them. An appeal body, consisting again of legal Commissioners, determined this appeal. It also reviewed annually all detention orders.

This attempt to introduce judicial overtones into the system was ill-fated. It was found to place an intolerable strain on the consciences of the lawyers who had to operate it, and who were properly reluctant to reach what seemed like a judicial decision without going through all the customary processes of public examination and cross-examination of witnesses. Inevitably, the lawyers insisted on substantial corroborative evidence before issuing an order, and this undoubtedly prevented the detention of many who, on security grounds, should have been detained. On the other hand, in spite of these precautions, it is foolish to claim that the system afforded to the accused the full benefit of a free trial. In practice, the average detainee could expect to be released, either by the *ex gratia* action of the Secretary of State who retained a full right to release whenever he chose, or on appeal to the Commissioners, within a year. When it is remembered that detention orders are often, in practice, sentences for murder, the system does not appear unduly oppressive. Its reform was accompanied by various measures designed to improve the possibility of convicting terrorists in the open courts by removing the right to trial by jury in certain categories of case, and by shifting the burden of proof in respect of certain types of evidence from the prosecution to the accused. Both of these methods had been introduced in Southern Ireland in 1972. The inadequate policing of Catholic areas, however, still makes detention the only weapon which can be normally relied on for the apprehension of Republican terrorists. Protestant terrorism, on the other hand, can more often be tried and punished by the courts.

In 1974 yet another Commission (this time under the ex-Labour Lord Chancellor, Lord Gardiner, a man well known for his liberal views) investigated the whole system again. He reached the conclusion once more that it was essential to keep detention. To the considerable dismay of many who had confidently expected the opposite conclusion from him, he went further by arguing that the elaborate safeguards set up under the Diplock proposals had proved inefficient and were objectionable on the general ground that they involved a confusion between justice and administration. Accordingly, he recommended a return to the purely administrative system of detention for the use of which Mr Faulkner had been so vehemently criticized in 1971. The Government has now adopted these proposals. What is certain is that, within months, Mr Maudling's decision to bring back internment, although it had proved politically advantageous to the IRA, had seriously damaged the IRA's military campaign. By the end of January 1972, the Army was claiming that the defeat of IRA terrorism in Belfast was now in sight: that once this was accomplished the Army could direct its full force on Londonderry and the Border areas, and that it was not absurdly optimistic to suppose that the IRA's campaign might collapse in little more than a year. It was at this stage, however, that another event, almost wholly accidental in its origins, intervened to divert the whole course of British policy, to end the Stormont Government and parliament, and to enable the IRA wholly to recoup its losses in Belfast, while converting the Catholic areas of Londonderry into a Republican fortress.

Chapter 8

Direct Rule

On 30 January 1972, the Northern Irish Civil Rights Association mounted a demonstration, attended by 20,000 people, in the Bogside and Creggan areas of Londonderry. These areas had been policed only intermittently since the troubles of 1969, and Army surveillance over them, though never wholly relaxed, had not prevented them from becoming veritable IRA fortresses. The authorities permitted the demonstration on condition that it was confined to this Republican territory. Towards the end of the proceedings, however, a number of demonstrators attacked the Army cordon in an effort to lead the march into Protestant Londonderry. The attempt was successfully resisted and the crowd began to retreat.

At this juncture, however, the security forces took a critical decision. Not content with containment, they pursued the retreating crowd into the Bogside for the purpose of arresting those who had been guilty of disorder. The inevitable consequence followed: IRA gunmen fired on the 'invading' force, and the soldiers returned fire. The result was a gun battle fought in the midst of a milling crowd. In the course of it, thirteen civilians were admitted by the Army to have been killed, a figure which Republicans claimed to be an underestimate.

It is not intended here to go into the merits of the detailed controversy about this operation which thereupon ensued. On the whole, the British press followed the almost invariable custom by reporting the event in a way strongly favourable to the rioters and extremely hostile to the Army. Later, the whole affair was investigated by an independent tribunal under Lord Chief Justice Widgery. Although its findings were promptly denounced by Republicans and Nationalists as grossly biased, two of them must surely command the assent of every sane critic—the initial responsibility for the disaster rested with those who had tried to start an illegal march, and the decision to launch an arrest operation (although fully justified in law and, indeed, in normal circumstances, a clear duty) may have been injudicious. The security forces had for long been under criticism for lack of zeal in making arrests on such occasions. A successful arrest operation in the heart of Republican Londonderry would have been a tonic to the spirits of all law-abiding Ulstermen and a crippling blow to IRA morale. In the event, however, the Army proved to have walked straight into an IRA trap set to capture, at the expense of civilian demonstrators, the British and Stormont Governments. The most familiar of terrorist techniques—the use of an apparently innocent protest demonstration as the shield for a gun attack on security forces, designed not primarily to injure them but to tempt them to action which could be misrepresented as the deliberate slaughter of the innocent—had worked to perfection. The Widgery Commission totally repudiated the suggestion that the Army had run amok, although it criticized some soldiers for behaviour bordering on the reckless; and it failed to find conclusive evidence that any of the thirteen were actually carrying guns or bombs at the time of their deaths.

In Dublin and in Catholic Ulster, however, there was no doubt what had happened in Londonderry on what was instantly elevated to an honoured place in the Republican calendar as 'Bloody Sunday'. The Army had fired ruthlessly on a fleeing crowd for the purpose of murdering peaceful, liberal protesters and innocent bystanders, discriminating particularly, as opportunity offered, against fresh-faced boys who might otherwise have lived to swell the ranks of patriotic militancy. The Dublin Government recalled its Ambassador; the Dublin mob burnt the British Embassy to the ground, and the SDLP made it clear that the last chance of any sort of compromise settlement in Ulster had gone. The British Labour Party was profoundly disturbed. Within days, the Tory Government had reached the conclusion that since a military operation which involved embarrassments on a scale as big as this was unendurable, all effort must now be concentrated on finding a political solution to Ulster's problem.

What had happened, in fact, was a repetition, albeit of an infinitely more dramatic and damaging character, of the exercise which had followed the two Londonderry deaths in July 1971. Those, although they arose from action by the Army for which the British Government was ultimately responsible, were used to justify the SDLP's withdrawal from Stormont, soon to be followed by the campaign for civil disobedience. In the same way, 'Bloody Sunday' was now used to compass the destruction of Stormont. For a few months, dating from the reintroduction of internment in the previous August, the British Government seemed to have reverted to the view that what it was engaged in in Ulster was a straightforward law-keeping operation for the defence of properly constituted authority. Mr Maudling, it appeared, had painfully reached the conclusion not only that a military solution was possible, but also that no other sort of solution was conceivable. This change of mood in Britain, if sustained, would have spelt doom to the IRA. It was imperative for the IRA to stop it by the traditional method of encouraging a crippling sensation of guilt in the British. Even on the most discreditable possible view of what had happened at Londonderry, the dismantling of Stormont could hardly appear to be a rational expiation. It is true that the Stormont Government was still theoretically responsible for security, and that Mr Faulkner still presided over the co-ordinating Security Committee, but it was known, and explicitly agreed, that the direction of military operations was in the hands of the GOC who was responsible to the Ministry of Defence. An attempt to punish Protestant Ulster for a tactical misjudgment by British Army commanders, or even for what was wildly alleged to be the murderous conduct of British troops, had neither justice nor prudence to commend it. This, however, was obviously not the conscious motive of the Government. Its reaction was the much more characteristic one that when war is seen to be un-endurable, diplomacy must be given its chance.

Within a few days of the Londonderry disaster, the political initiative which it had been engineered to prompt had begun. On 4 February 1972 Mr Faulkner met Mr Heath and it was decided that the two Governments should separately work out their plans for a comprehensive and pacific settlement in Ulster. These plans would later be compared and might provide, it was hoped, the basis of an agreement. The area within which com-promise had to be sought was delimited at one end by the SDLP's demand for the end of internment and the transfer (at the very least) of total responsibility for internal security from Stormont to Whitehall and, at the other, by Mr Faulkner's determination to maintain intact the degree of devolution which Stormont enjoyed, and not to abandon internment until the state of security justified doing so. Their followed, for six weeks, what looked like a long-distance game of poker between Stormont and

Whitehall, during which there was virtually no direct contact between the two Governments. As the Cabinet's discussions proceeded in London, however, a spate of rumours about what was being designed for Ulster was unleashed, and many of these rumours were known to have originated in very high places. Some talked of an outright decision to abolish Stormont; others affirmed that the British Government would certainly be content with nothing less than the permanent transfer to Whitehall of the control of the RUC. There were suggestions of direct rule from a Northern Irish Office in London, suggestions that some sort of 'supremo' would be despatched to Belfast with a more or less limitless remit, and suggestions that a Commission of prominent Catholics and Protestants would be installed to govern the Province until its institutions could be reconstructed. Stormont was clearly being subjected to a deliberate war of nerves, and at one point the feeling arose that the pressure was being increased beyond the limits of prudence. Accordingly, Mr Heath sent a telegram to Mr Faulkner for the comfort of Ulster Unionists, affirming that wild speculations about the British Government's intentions should be ignored, a gesture which was later to be cited as one of the cruellest instances of the Government's perfidy.

By the end of March, Mr Faulkner's Government had completed its own list of proposals. It suggested that, while constitutional responsibility for internal security should remain with Stormont, a permanent British Government representative, possibly of ministerial rank, should be added to the security committee in Belfast. On internment, Mr Faulkner reiterated his commitment to phase it out as order was progressively restored and to abolish altogether the Emergency Powers Act. While not accepting proportional representation for Stormont, he drew attention to the Unionist party's scheme for enlarging the Northern Ireland House of Commons in order to bring about increased representation, and he left the door open for the reconsideration of proportional representation. Most strikingly of all, however, he included two concessions to the demand for an 'Irish dimension'. He proposed a common law enforcement area for the whole of Ireland and the eventual creation of an inter-governmental Council of Ireland. Plainly, Faulkner had concluded that the time for hard bargaining was over. He had contrived a scheme which went to the very limits of what was politically possible for a Unionist Prime Minister to suggest, in

86

the mood of Northern Irish opinion as it then was, without ensuring his own instant dismissal. When he flew to London on 22 March to present these proposals, however, he found that the British Cabinet was adamant for the one concession which he could not give—the transfer, seemingly on a permanent basis, of the responsibility for internal Northern Irish security to Westminster. When Faulkner returned to Belfast, he found his Cabinet, with the exception of one dissident (curiously enough, the hardliner Mr Harry West), unanimously resolved to reject the British proposal. He flew back to London to report this decision and was told, as he had already been warned, that Britain would immediately introduce legislation for the prorogation of Stormont and the establishment of direct rule. It was left only for the entire Northern Irish Cabinet, including Mr West, to give its resignation to the Governor and for the Parliament at Westminster to rush through in twenty-four hours a Bill, putting the Northern Ireland constitution in cold storage, initially for a year but with the provision that the period could be extended by an Order-in-Council. This Bill received the Royal Assent on 1 April, a date which Unionists, in their lighter moments, like to emphasize.

Faulkner himself had been wholly taken by surprise. He had maintained for months, in the face of the pessimism of many of his colleagues and advisers, that the British Government would in the last resort shrink from what seemed to him to be the ultimate act of folly. The reaction in Northern Ireland generally was instant and dramatic. A vast but highly disciplined Protestant crowd marched from Belfast to Stormont to express its undying loyalty to the Parliament which fifty years earlier Unionists had accepted only as a 'supreme sacrifice', but which had come to be regarded as the last surviving barrier against British betrayal. This gesture was followed by a token one-day Loyalist strike.

Whether the British Government had in fact foreseen that its demand for the control of internal security would be rejected, with the consequence that direct rule would become inevitable, remains something of a mystery. One fact is certain, however: no one with even the most superficial knowledge of Northern Irish Unionist politics at this juncture could have doubted the outcome. The British Government had taken pains to keep itself closely advised about all fluctuations in Northern Irish opinion and, though the perceptiveness of its chief adviser, Mr Howard Smith (the Government's resident representative in

Belfast), has never been beyond question, it seems unlikely that the absolute opposition of Unionists to surrender on the security issue could have escaped his observation. Faulkner's decision to go, rather than to allow Stormont's powers to be attenuated in the middle of a civil war, had the total support of the Parliamentary party and the party in the country. Had he decided otherwise, he would instantly have been sacked and condemned to perpetual ignominy. The probability is, therefore, that the majority of the British Cabinet had reached the conclusion that nothing less than a simple and sweeping gesture, designed to gratify the most cherished of immediate Republican aspirations, would suffice to win over the Catholic population to active co-operation in the defeat of terrorism.

The one substantial argument in the eyes of British Ministers against direct rule was the fear that it might prompt an actual Protestant rebellion. This objection, however, had been diligently anticipated over several months by the reports of British civil servants who, even while the SDLP's sulk was at its height, had maintained the closest relations with Catholic politicians. From these politicians they had learnt that 'the Protestant backlash' was and always had been a myth. Some doubt on this point had been stirred by the appearance early in the year of William Craig's Vanguard Movement, which evoked the memory of Carson's volunteers and which held well-attended rallies at which the language of rebellion was freely used. In spite of its militaristic vocabulary, however, Vanguard still seemed to be an essentially pacific protest movement. Nevertheless no one who was in Belfast at the time could doubt that if any political leader of influence had given the smallest encouragement to Protestant violence the Province would have been in flames. Indeed, more than absence of encouragement was needed to prevent that calamity. It was essential that Protestant political leaders, while urging physical restraint, should do their best to express the outraged feelings of their supporters. Mr Faulkner realized this, and when he heard that Craig proposed to address the crowd outside Stormont, he wisely agreed to appear on the balcony with him and made a speech which showed that the leader of Vanguard, though one of Ulster's principal political extremists, could not claim a monopoly of resentment against the British. Incredibly, the significance of this gesture was totally misunderstood in Britain. It was taken there as showing that Faulkner was himself an extremist prepared to fraternize with the champions of counter-revolution. Justice demands that it should be recordep here that Paisley also played a valuable stabilizing part by urging his supporters to refrain from violence.

The imposition of direct rule signified the abandonment by the British Government of the theory that the Army was simply in Northern Ireland for the purpose of offering aid to the civil power, of defending legally established institutions against terrorist attack. The alternative theory, which had always lived uneasily alongside it, was that Britain had assumed a custodial role, that she was in Ulster not merely to restore order but to reshape the Province's system of government. The transition to this view of the nature of British intervention had several important and obvious consequences. In the first place, it represented a victory for violence. That, of course, was not the intention of the British Government: its intention was to offer a bribe to moderate Catholic political opinion, to show that Mr Fitt and Mr Hume had achieved by peaceful means more than the IRA could achieve by bombing. No one, however, who looked at the facts could conceivably reach this last conclusion. Nationalist politicians had hated Stormont for fifty years, with only occasional intervals of relative goodwill; yet Stormont had endured. It was clear to the meanest intelligence that what had brought about the dismantling of this majestic structure was not the diplomacy (such as it was) of the SDLP, but the activity of the IRA. Another consequence was to deprive the Protestant majority in Northern Ireland of all constitutional outlets for the expression of its mounting grievances. Clearly, this must lead at the very least to the formation of extra-constitutional movements which, when the provocation became greater, would develop into paramilitary movements. Political parties live by regular political conflict which has as its aim the attainment or retention of office. Remove this aim by abolishing the constitution, and the interminable, gruelling activity—the organizing of meetings, the publication of pamphlets, the holding of bazaars—in which day-to-day politics largely consists cannot easily be maintained. Before direct rule, Faulkner still presided over a fundamentally united Unionist party which he was still successfully leading along a path of reform which a few years earlier would have seemed Utopian. With Stormont gone, he was to find it increasingly difficult to maintain the party's cohesion. Salaried politicians with nothing to do rapidly become turbulent. Within a few months, distinguished members of the party's Left were withdrawing in protest against Faulkner's allegedly anti-British stance. The Right was even more dissatisfied, contending unreasonably that earlier firmness on Faulkner's part would have averted catastrophe. The only surviving parliamentary representative of the Northern Irish people—the Ulster Unionist group at Westminster under Captain Lawrence Orr—suffered from remoteness, and from the suspicion with which it had become customary to regard Ulster's Westminster politicians. The competition between them and Faulkner for the role of spokesman for Unionist Ulster was destined to become yet another source of Unionist dissension. The only possible beneficiaries of this Unionist disintegration could be those Protestant politicians who were at home in the streets rather than in Parliament.

Added to all this there was now a general atmosphere of uncertainty. Direct rule was in itself a policy with no positive content. It could be used, for instance, to mount a Draconian military campaign against the IRA. A few Unionists comforted themselves for a while with the thought that this might be the subtle intention of the British Government. Britain, it was said, had been inhibited by the feeling, unjustifiable though it was, that she was being required to defend an oppressive political system in Ulster. Now that this encumbrance was removed, she would be able to throw herself wholeheartedly into the battle. Direct rule was itself a retort to all charges of discrimination. Once the authority being assailed in Ulster was manifestly the Westminster Parliament, not a Unionist *junta* in Belfast, it should become easier to rally the loyal elements in the Catholic population. Moreover, Britain would learn by her own bitter experience the kind of toughness always needed to govern Ulster.

These wishful thoughts, however, were confined to a very few and they were almost instantly rendered unthinkable by the stance assumed by the new Secretary of State for Northern Ireland, Mr William Whitelaw, who took over responsibility for the Province from the Home Secretary. William Whitelaw had achieved prominence at Westminster as a Chief Whip and later as Leader of the House of Commons. The demands which both these offices make are on tactical rather than strategic qualities. He had the reputation of a man who, by a combination of infinite personal charm, obvious humanity, extreme flexibility and a total lack of interest in abstract principles, could usually succeed in getting most of his own (or more precisely, most of his master's) way. He was certainly not given to long-term planning, but in so far as his political career to date had given any evidence of a persistent inclination, it was an inclination towards concession. He, it was said, had been largely responsible for persuading his colleagues away from the relatively stern free-market policies on which they had been elected in Britain. He, it was believed, had played a leading part in advocating in the Cabinet a thorough-going political initiative in Ulster. His admirers said that his reconciling qualities were almost magical, that a few words from Willie would soften even the rockiest of Ulster hearts and that no conflict of principle could fail to yield to the benign influence which his very presence generated. IRA violence in the Province had, of course, been stepped up while the British and Stormont Governments were formulating their proposals. It had even spread to England on 22 February when an IRA bomb in an Army canteen at Aldershot killed seven people. In Ulster, passion had been particularly aroused by the planting of a bomb in March in a restaurant full of women and children. On this last occasion, there were two deaths and 130 injuries, many of them serious and permanent. After direct rule there was no falling-off in violence but this did not prevent Mr Whitelaw from embarking at once on the policy of phasing out internment. Substantial releases were made as a gesture of goodwill.

The most serious consequence of the deterioration in security which had set in immediately after 'Bloody Sunday' was the appearance of genuinely 'no-go' areas. The Bogside and the Creggan were now protected by armed IRA barricades. In Belfast, where, in the course of 1971, the Army and the military police had succeeded in making themselves felt in the Catholic areas, the barricades had now also gone up again. There were large areas in the Province in which ordinary law enforcement was recognized as impossible, which troops could not patrol save in motorized vehicles at high speed, and where the IRA was free to store arms, drill men and enforce its own discipline through 'kangaroo' courts and by such methods as tarring and feathering, knee-capping and, when thought necessary, actual murder.

By June, the Protestant populace of Belfast was reaching the limit of its endurance. Protestant para-military movements, the chief of which was the Ulster Defence Association, were daily increasing in importance. So far, Mr Whitelaw's pacific energies had been concentrated almost exclusively on the Republicans. He had made it clear that only in the very last resort would he be prepared to use military force to end the no-go areas. His aides did not flinch from assuring visiting journalists that any such operation would lead to at least a thousand fatal casualties, most of whom, it was confidently opined, would be nursing mothers and young children. Competent military and police opinion at the time varied between estimates of one or two, and twenty fatal casualties for the reoccupation of Republican London derry. Clearly, however, the British Government was not letting itself in for another 'Bloody Sunday'.

Instead, Mr Whitelaw set out to charm the Republican barricades down. He gave tea parties for Bogside ladies who assured him that they wanted peace, although some were prone to add that the IRA boys meant no real harm. Republican propaganda continued to insist on a complete ending of internment and the granting of a total amnesty as essential conditions for the return of normal policing. Nevertheless, Mr Whitelaw had the occasional success: barricades were an inconvenience to Londonderry housewives and from time to time some of them were removed, only to be replaced later. These operations could take place safely since it was obvious that the authorities would not attempt any snap invasion of the no-go territories. Undoubtedly, however, Mr Whitelaw was achieving, with the unwitting help of the IRA, some small and local successes. A referendum conducted by the IRA in June in the Bogside and Creggan areas failed to produce a very impressive majority for IRA aims, in spite of intimidation and the fact that the votes were counted by IRA men. There was a feeling among some Republicans that the British Government was now embarked upon a path of limitless concession, and the need for violence had accordingly diminished. What Mr Whitelaw did not allow for was that, so long as the no-go areas survived, the IRA would be able to nip in the bud, by brutal and effective means, any practical expression of Catholic goodwill towards the Government's initiative.

By mid-June, Protestant patience was nearing exhaustion and Mr Whitelaw was obliged to direct his charm to the majority rather than the minority. An IRA suggestion of a negotiated truce was brusquely and high-mindedly turned down. The UDA indicated that, if a date were not given for the end of Catholic no-go areas, it would put up its own barricades and establish its own no-go areas in Belfast. Mr Whitelaw met the Protestant para-military leaders and achieved a staggering success in momentarily soothing them. Hope began to rise that the British Government might already have perceived the limits of possible appeasement and that the 'initiative' might be about to take a new turn. Within a week, however, these hopes were shattered by a move which, in the gravity of its consequences, was arguably the worst blunder committed in the course of the Ulster crisis and, some would say, ranks among the classic blunders of political history.

On 22 June the Provisional IRA announced that it would suspend offensive action provided that a suitable reciprocal response was forthcoming from the forces of the Crown. Mr Whitelaw declared in the House of Commons that since those forces were present in Northern Ireland for the purpose of suppressing violence, any cessation of IRA hostilities would naturally be reflected in the Army's behaviour. In effect, this was the promise of an even lower 'profile' than the Army had hitherto displayed since the beginning of direct rule. In theory, this was not a negotiated truce (a formula which was later to become familiar). The IRA had suspended action of its own volition, although in the stated expectation of a suitable response. The British Government had, equally of its own volition and without undertaking any conditions, announced its intention of supplying that response. The British conscience which, contrary to popular belief, is given to casuistry, was wholly satisfied with the arrangement. Mr Whitelaw had not departed from the principle of not talking to terrorists; he had simply exchanged silent signals with them at a decorous distance.

To the less sophisticated Protestant Northern Irish mind, however, the event was traumatic. The British Government had manifestly done a deal with the terrorists. The nature of that deal soon became apparent in the speeding up in the releases of internees and the suspension of all Army activity likely to endanger the truce. Plainly, there could now be no thought of an invasion of the no-go areas. The reaction of the Protestant para-military movements was swift and predictable: the Protestant barricades went up in Belfast. The spectacle of masked UDA men guarding the entrances to Protestant areas and conducting patrols became familiar. Rapidly, it became apparent that Ulster had come nearer than ever before to a total suspension of lawful authority. The much advertised 'polarization of the community' had at last become a reality. The real centres of power throughout a large part of the community were now the para-military movements, Provisional or Protestant. It was also clear that the initiative had acquired an entirely new theme. The original aim of

British policy was supposed to have been the detachment of moderate Catholic opinion from relatively benevolent neutrality towards the IRA to active co-operation with the security forces; it seemed that this had been abandoned overnight. Instead, Mr Whitelaw was now seeking a direct deal with the IRA. Such a deal, if it was to be permanent, could only be made at the expense of moderate Catholic politicians. The SDLP which, at this juncture, was in a parlous state of isolation—still committed to have nothing to do with the British Government until the last internee was released, and still subject to constant threats from the IRA—did not oppose the truce. Almost anything which temporarily relieved the pressure from which it was suffering would have been welcome to it. Privately, however, much anxiety was expressed about the possibility that Britain would strike a lasting bargain with the terrorists over the heads of constitutional Catholics. That anxiety was also felt in Dublin. The suspicion that, for all their vaunted idealism and moderation, what the British really respected was power, was now freely expressed.

The truce began at midnight on 26 June, being preceded by a number of actions to make the point that the IRA was parleying from strength not weakness. It lasted for thirteen days. Throughout this period, murders continued and fatal casualties, during the armistice, amounted to seventeen. By Friday, 7 July, it seemed evident that the battle was about to be resumed; the truce had served its function. It had given the Provisionals a welcome breathing space for reorganization and it had secured the release of a considerable number of internees who were now free to return to the front lines. There was no shortage of occasions for ending it. A propitious one was provided by a dispute in Belfast over the allocation of sixteen empty houses in the no-man's-land between a Catholic and a Protestant area at Lenadoon. The failure of Mr Whitelaw's gamble now seemed assured. His stake, however, was too high to encourage him to write off his losses without making one desperate effort to save the day. The truce, although it seemed at the time to have lost for him for ever the respect and trust of the Protestant community in Ulster, had been naïvely hailed in Britain as another example of his miraculous diplomatic gifts. What is more, he had a genuine passion for peace. He undoubtedly believed that it would be immoral to sacrifice any chance of sparing Ulster a full-scale resumption of the terrorist campaign.

All this led him to commit what he himself is reported later to have admitted (with characteristic honesty) to be a blunder, and what many regard as his supreme blunder. Snatching at straws, he invited a delegation of Provisional leaders (led by Seamus Twomey, the arch-IRA terrorist and head of the Belfast brigade) to come to London with safe-conducts for the purpose of discussing with him means of maintaining the truce. The IRA presented its traditional demands—the end of internment, withdrawal of troops, and a declaration of intent to dissolve the Union. Mr Whitelaw, although not encouraging them to expect the concession of any of these demands, tried to postpone the inevitable conclusion by agreeing to report them to his Cabinet colleagues. But even this was not enough for the Provisionals. They returned to Belfast resolved to end the truce. On the following Sunday (9 July), IRA agitators easily succeeded in staging a riot over the disputed Lenadoon houses. The Army had to use rubber bullets and the IRA had its pretext for resuming hostilities.

The immediate consequences of this abortive interlude were two: the state of security in Northern Ireland had vastly deteriorated and Mr Whitelaw's moral authority over the Protestant community had seemingly been totally extinguished. The deterioration arose not only from the fact that the IRA was much stronger than it had been at the beginning of the truce, but also from the fact that Protestant militancy was now much more formidable and blatant than it had ever been before. The UDA, a powerful and still relatively disciplined force, appeared publicly on the streets, hijacked cars when these were required for its operations and gave frequent television interviews. In mid-July 1972, Ulster came nearer to displaying the character of a country without government than it had ever done before. In Protestant eyes, Mr Whitelaw had forfeited the right to take a strong line against Protestant rebellion by his acquiescence in the Republican rebellion. It seemed incredible that his mission in Ulster could be continued.

By the end of the month, however, he had accomplished a staggering recovery. He showed himself to be possessed of that limitless capacity for prompt adaptations to changed conditions which is the strength of his type in politics. The flirtation with the IRA was over; it had manifestly failed and was clearly a mistake not to be repeated. Given these facts, it was essential as rapidly as possible to end the no-go areas and to revert to the task of reconstructing the Northern Irish constitution in a manner which would be acceptable to moderate Catholics and bearable to the Protestant majority. The immediate need was to disarm Protestant hostility.

In the early hours of 31 July the Army, in a carefully prepared operation based on massive force and the use of tanks, invaded the no-go areas of Belfast and Londonderry. That desperate operation from which Mr Whitelaw and his advisers had so far shrunk, maintaining that it would involve a holocaust by comparison with which 'Bloody Sunday' would pale into insignificance, was accomplished in the face of virtually no resistance and with a loss, in a shooting incident in Londonderry following the occupation, of only two lives. Mr Whitelaw argued that the humane success was due to the months of concessions which, he said, had destroyed popular support for the IRA in the no-go areas. Others pointed out that they had always predicted that a properly prepared operation would pass off precisely as this one had done. In the euphoria which followed the end of no-go, however, almost everybody was prepared to give the Secretary of State the benefit of the doubt. The Protestants began spontaneously to remove their own barricades. Their action, they contended, had always been defensive in character: with the end of Republican no-go, there was no need for Protestant no-go. The British had learnt the lesson that compromise with the IRA was impossible. With that firmly established, the task of constructing Ulster's future could be begun. Against all probabilities, Mr Whitelaw was back in the saddle, this time with more Protestant confidence than he had ever had before.

Chapter 9

Faulkner: Mark II

Operation 'Motorman'—the reoccupation of the no-go areas—laid the foundation for the political reconstruction on which Mr Whitelaw was to embark in 1973. There was an immediate and sustained improvement in security. The Army was now free to go where it liked; there were no areas in which the police, if accompanied by suitable military protection, could not at least make a formal appearance. Fear among the Protestants of a British 'sell-out' though always present began to diminish. It seemed that the British Government had at least grasped the truth that security must come first, that any political settlement would be vitiated if it came into being against a background of growing public disorder.

The British Government also seemed to have grasped some other truths. It began to see Mr Faulkner not as hitherto, as a wily, calculating but fundamentally uncompromising Unionist hardliner, but rather as the key to the hearts of the Protestant majority, and the most valuable British asset in Ulster. Since the SDLP, responding to the new atmosphere, had, by painful and reluctant degrees, now reached the conclusion that it could write if not actually talk to British politicians even before the last internee was released, the wind seemed to be set fair for a compromise settlement based on that beloved British panacea, the political centre.

Mr Whitelaw summoned a conference of Northern Irish political parties at Darlington, County Durham. Each was invited to submit its own proposals for the future constitution of Northern Ireland, and although members of the SDLP were not physically present, they complied with this request. The conference did no more than define the area of disagreement, which was vast, but it served its purpose, which was to supply Mr Whitelaw with the material out of which he could construct his own constitutional blueprint.

The first need, however, was thoroughly to banish from Unionist minds the suspicion that all these complicated exercises in constitution-making were in reality nothing but an elaborate façade behind which Britain was preparing to coerce or manœuvre Ulster into a united Ireland. Unionists had for long been demanding a plebiscite on the Border and Mr Heath had already promised this to them. They now stridently demanded that the promise should be fulfilled. It was not easy for the British mind to grasp the importance which Ulster Protestants attached to this plebiscite. The facts were already available; roughly two thirds of Ulster was Protestant, and that two thirds, with a few eccentric exceptions, was known to be bent on maintaining the Union with Britain. There was more doubt about the precise number of Catholics who actually favoured unification with the South, but, in the atmosphere of 1973 and with IRA intimidation, a factor which could still not be ignored, it was fair to assume that the Catholic population would either abstain from voting (as the SDLP urged them to) or vote for Irish unity. No staggering revelation could therefore be expected from the plebiscite.

Nevertheless, it was psychologically of the highest importance. An overwhelming vote for the preservation of the Union would lay on record before the whole world the fact which must provide the framework for any future constitution—the fact that Ulster was and would remain a part of the United Kingdom. Not only would this make any British surrender more difficult, it would establish before the outside world (which was extremely confused about Ulster) the British Government's credentials for its law-keeping role in the Province. IRA propaganda had been singularly successful in spreading abroad the impression that Britain was engaged in a colonialist campaign in Ulster, that her Army was an army of occupation and that she was bent on denying the right of self-determination to the Irish people.

Accordingly, on 8 March, a Border Poll offering Ulster the choice between continued membership of the United Kingdom and membership of a united Ireland was held. Approximately 58 per cent voted for the preservation of the Union with Britain and only about 1 per cent for a united Ireland, the remaining 41 per cent abstaining. The result was at least satisfactory to the Unionists and, when measured against normal voting habits and with due allowance made for electoral lethargy, it could be argued to show that at least some Catholics had opted for the British yoke. This cleared the way for Mr Whitelaw's constitutional proposals.

These appeared in a White Paper on 21 March. The essentials of the scheme consisted of three proposals—for a legislative assembly (to include eighty members) elected by proportional representation, with large powers over all matters of home policy except security and the franchise; eventual creation of some sort of consultative Council of Ireland, and a series of measures designed to guarantee still further civil rights. This left open the two volcanic areas of disagreement where the opposing positions of Unionists and Republicans appeared inherently irreconcilable—the question of how the regional Executive should be formed with a view to the demand for power-sharing, and the question of who, in the future, would be responsible for internal security. Confronted with these insoluble dilemmas, the White Paper prevaricated in a manner which made it possible for both sides of the dispute to go on talking without loss of face or surrender of principle. As to the Executive, it was proposed that the elected Assembly should itself devise the system by which Ministers should be appointed and government conducted. However, the Secretary of State should refrain from devolving any legislative powers to the Assembly until he was satisfied that the system which it had devised met the British Government's requirements.

Two crucial passages defined the criteria by which the Secretary of State was to reach that decision: the first read: 'It is the view of the Government that the Executive itself can no longer be solely based upon any single party, if that party draws its support and its elected representation virtually entirely from only one section of a divided community.' The second stipulated that: 'Executive powers will not be concentrated in elected representatives from one community only.'

Here, then, was Mr Whitelaw's attempt to reconcile the SDLP's demands for a power-sharing Executive with the Unionists' insistence on majority rule, exercised in the British way, through a collectively responsible Cabinet. The SDLP favoured proportional representation in government; that is to say, a system under which every party elected to the Assembly would have a number of seats in government corresponding to its strength in the Assembly. This the Unionists had utterly rejected on the ground that it would produce political chaos and make cabinet government impossible. They also suspected (as history entitled them to) that SDLP politicians, who inherited the abstentionist attitudes of their Nationalist and Republican forbears, would use any representation they might get in government to promote the cause of Irish unity where necessary by the ruthless obstruction of business. Mr Whitelaw, it should be observed, was careful not to rule out the device of proportional representation in government. If the Unionists would swallow it, all well and good. On the other hand, his criteria would not rule out a Unionist administration which could prove that it had substantial Catholic electoral support and which included some Catholics in its membership. Such an administration was still a daydream which ran counter to all the traditions and habits of Northern Irish politics. However, a coalition between Unionists and members of the new Alliance party (which was partly Catholic in composition) was by no means out of the question. This, if it could come into being, would surely meet the Secretary of State's requirements.

Here, then, was a characteristic example of Mr Whitelaw's diplomacy: Mr Faulkner could accept the White Paper, at least as a basis for discussion, without committing himself to forming an Executive with the SDLP. Such a commitment would have been lethal to him. It would have involved the betrayal of his promise not to collaborate with those whose primary aim was the destruction of the Union. A political alliance between Unionists and a party which, like the SDLP, was engaged in passive resistance to the State was still politically impossible. Equally, the SDLP could accept Mr Whitelaw's White Paper in principle without renouncing its own constitutional proposals.

The same evasive tactics were applied to the equally nettled question of where the responsibility for the control of the Northern Irish police was eventually to rest. For the moment, the White Paper declared, it would remain at Westminster. That was a disappointment for the Unionists but one for which they were prepared and which could be justified on the view that Westminster control was a necessary consequence of the emergency. The White Paper held out hopes, however, that when peace had returned and the new 'non-sectarian' constitution was operating smoothly, responsibility for internal security might be given to the Assembly. The Assembly would then be virtually a reproduction of Stormont with the important difference that it would be elected by proportional representation (which would automatically ensure a larger representation of Catholic parties), and that it would be led by an Executive in which, by some means yet to be specified, some Catholics would always be included.

From the Unionist point of view, however, the White Paper had one fatal flaw. It was proposed that Northern Ireland should be deprived of its Governor. The office of Governor, through which the Queen was represented to her Northern Irish subjects, was an object of something closely approaching veneration to the Protestant population. The argument that the Governor was a mere mediator between the Queen and her loyal subjects and that in future Her Majesty herself would have a direct relationship with them which could be cemented, when times were better, by frequent royal visits to the Province, did nothing to assuage Unionist resentment. This was all the stronger because the current tenant of the office, Lord Grey of Naunton, was deeply admired for his personal qualities. The Unionist reaction on this point was far from purely emotional. The fact that Northern Ireland had a Governor whose formal functions under the old constitution had been in relation to Stormont what the Queen's functions are in relation to Parliament had come to be regarded as a guarantee of that degree of local independence to which the Province was entitled by law and custom. It had been the business of the Governor to give his assent to Acts of the Northern Irish Parliament, to appoint Ministers at the recommendation of the Northern Irish Prime Minister, and to grant dissolutions at that Prime Minister's request. The suspicion was that, once the Governor had gone, these formal functions would become vested in the Secretary of State and would in fact cease to be purely formal. Ministerial appointments would have actually, not merely theoretically, to be approved by Whitehall; Acts of the Assembly would have really to win approval from the British Government if they were to pass into law; the Assembly would exist only at the pleasure of the Secretary of State who would be able to prorogue or dissolve it whenever he liked. Northern Ireland would thereby be denied both the advantages of total integration (the White Paper made no provision for a proper increase in Ulster representation at Westminster designed to bring it up to the level enjoyed by Scotland), and those of entrenched local autonomy in certain spheres.

In the event, these fears proved entirely correct. When the new constitutional Act, embodying the provisions of the White Paper, received the Royal Assent in mid-summer, the Secretary of State's powers were found to be as large as the critics had predicted they would be. When the White Paper was published, however, it seemed reasonable to suppose that Mr Whitelaw would have taken the elementary precaution of including in it at least some demands unacceptable to the Unionists by way of a normal bargaining tactic; these contentious items would then be available for concessions during the negotiations. Many felt that the proposal to abolish the Governor might turn out to have been one such demand. If, after strenuous protests from Mr Faulkner, this point had been dropped, Mr Whitelaw would have been seen as a man sensitive to Unionist feeling, and Mr Faulkner's reputation as an efficient guardian of Unionist interests would also have benefited. Mr Whitelaw's subtlety, however, is not so Machiavellian. The months that followed showed that, although now conscious of the value of Mr Faulkner to British policy, the British Government was still obsessed with the view that its interests lay in pushing him as far as possible. They also showed that Mr Faulkner, although he had started the year in a relatively strong position *vis-à-vis* his own supporters, was fundamentally convinced that he had no real alternative but to allow himself to be pushed. The interaction of these two men during the next twelve months proved disastrous to the policies of both. The melancholy tale can best be told by examining a series of major blunders which Mr Faulkner, now firmly under the Whitelaw spell, proceeded to commit.

Having examined the White Paper, Mr Faulkner declared that he would accept it subject to certain reservations which could now be discussed. The SDLP said roughly the same thing. In this initial decision, Mr Faulkner was undoubtedly right. The White Paper contained nothing necessarily incompatible with his principles since, on the two subjects of power-sharing with Republicans and control of internal security, it had to be calculatedly vague. Inevitably, the decision to give even qualified acceptance to the document outraged the Paisleyites and the Craigites, but they were already lost to the Unionist party. Inevitably, also, it disturbed Mr Faulkner's Right wing supporters. Most of them still felt, however, that, given enough firmness in future negotiations, the essentials of the Unionist position could be defended. The first of the issues which called for such firmness was that of the Governor. A group of Mr Faulkner's closest supporters, including one of the shrewdest and most loyal of them, Captain John Brooke, now Lord Brookeborough (son of the former Prime Minister), begged Mr Faulkner to be intransient on this point. These imprecations had some success in that the Unionist Women's Council organized a petition on the subject; it was left to Paisley, Craig and the 'Loyalists', however, to lead the campaign on this highly emotive and popular question. Mr Faulkner regretted the Governor's departure but was not prepared to do overmuch about it, and in this he displayed two of his weaknesses—a certain lack of sensitivity in relation to issues with a romantic rather than a purely rational appeal, and an insufficient interest in constitutional problems. A practical man, he showed more interest in getting things done than in the processes by which they are done.

Having made this initial mistake, Mr Faulkner set about preparing himself for the forthcoming elections. There were to be local elections at the end of May (that is to say, elections for the newly designed local authorities which in future were to have only modest powers) and Assembly elections at the end of June. The most serious problem with which Mr Faulkner was going to be confronted when the Assembly met was that of power-sharing. It seemed that the vast majority of his supporters in the country, and indeed most of his political colleagues, were still irrevocably opposed to the idea of forming an administration with the SDLP with its Nationalist and Republican aims. It could be powerfully argued that Mr Faulkner was morally committed never to do any such thing. His best hope, therefore, was an election result which would enable him to form a coalition with the Alliance party. Any such coalition before the election was out of the question, since it would alienate Mr Faulkner's already troubled Right wing. Nevertheless, the return of a substantial number of Alliance candidates to the Assembly could be nothing but of advantage to the Unionists since it would enable them to form an Executive which would be satisfactory to Mr Whitelaw. Mr Faulkner's main preoccupation should have been to contain his own Unionist Right by advocating policies noticeably tougher than those of Alliance or at any rate using language more consonant with Unionist tradition.

By contrast, Mr Faulkner seemed to be obsessed at this time with two quite different considerations. He believed that Alliance was a threat to him because of its enlightened and modern attitudes which, he was unaccountably convinced, had become extremely popular among Unionists. This impression arose partly from the number of eminent Unionist desertions, notably that of Sir Robert Porter, former Minister for Home Affairs, to the

Alliance cause. It was also confirmed by the dubious results of a local opinion poll, and it seemed to be reinforced by the relative success of Alliance candidates at the local elections at the end of May. Mr Faulkner told his close Unionist supporters in effect that they must compete with Alliance in welcoming the British initiative, since otherwise they might lose a substantial number of seats to this party. The possibility of Left-wing Unionist desertion certainly did exist, but it was not very serious nor, under proportional representation, was the danger of split Protestant votes. What matters, however, is that it would have profited Mr Faulkner more to lose his Left to Alliance than to lose his Right to Paisley and Craig.

This truth was probably obscured from Mr Faulkner by his growing and understandable obsession with the danger of becoming a prisoner of a Right-wing dominated party. He had the best reasons for knowing what that could mean to a liberal Prime Minister; he had, after all, been the leader of the Right-wing rebels under O'Neill. What he does not seem to have realized, however, was the delicate and confused state of even much moderate Unionist opinion. Even loyal supporters were baffled by the White Paper. They wanted to see the Unionist party led by a man who would strike a tough bargain on their behalf. In this respect, they were beginning to lose confidence in Brian Faulkner, although many of them were still doing so with the utmost reluctance. The party needed coaxing and reassuring, instead of which Mr Faulkner decided to discipline it. He would have no truck with Unionist candidates for the Assembly elections who would not sign a pledge to support his entire manifesto, and it was the introduction of this pledge which proved utterly disastrous for him. It drove many into unwilling rebellion.

Mr Faulkner had always suffered from a certain aloofness from his colleagues and their advice. There were powerful Unionists, like the Reverend Martin Smyth (head of the Orange Order in Ireland), whose support was crucial to him. Many of them were not so stern and inflexible as they looked; some of them would have been flattered to have their opinion occasionally asked, but Mr Faulkner shrank from close contact with those with whom he felt no instinctive sympathy. The barrier which grew up at this time between him and the orthodox Unionist Right (particularly that section of it which sat under Captain Orr at Westminster) eventually proved fatal to him.

Mr Faulkner's Unionists and the Alliance party had both done relatively well in the May local elections; the SDLP had done surprisingly badly and the various 'Loyalist' groups had no great cause for self-congratulation. The results of the Assembly elections, however, proved surprisingly different. The Faulkner Unionists secured only twenty-two seats (one of which was almost immediately rendered vacant by a fatal motor accident), unpledged Unionists captured ten seats, Paisleyites and Craigites together fifteen, other 'loyalists' three, the SDLP nineteen, the Alliance party eight and the Northern Irish Labour party one. It took an optimist on Mr Faulkner's own scale to see these results as anything but a moral victory for the dissident Unionist Right. Worse still, however, they made it clear that if an Executive was to be formed at all Mr Faulkner would have to accept the SDLP as colleagues. This, it seemed certain, would finally outrage the great majority of his supporters in the country.

Mr Faulkner, however, is nothing if not resilient. It did not take too great a feat of casuistry for him to maintain that his commitment was not to shun all collaboration with the SDLP but merely to shun all collaboration with those whose 'primary aim' was the unification of Ireland on the basis of a Republican constitution. If the SDLP could convince Unionists that they were no longer in this category, the day might yet be saved. Mr Whitelaw would surely have some interest in persuading them to do so. If Mr Faulkner could say that he was merely forming an emergency coalition with the SDLP to carry out an agreed, immediate—and much needed—social and economic programme, and if he could establish that the SDLP (still engaged in a rent-and-rates strike) was now thoroughly loyal to the constitution, he might get away with it. This required, however, a certain degree of flexibility on the part of the SDLP.

That party had already received unspeakable boons. The new PR system of elections ensured it of powerful representation in the Assembly; it was clearly about to be given a place in government; it had even exacted a tribute to the Irish dimension in the shape of a promise to set up an all-Ireland consultative council. If it pressed for more, it would alienate the entire Protestant community, and what would its life in Ulster be worth then? With a *Fine Gael* Government in power in Dublin, there was every chance that it would no longer receive enthusiastic support from that quarter on which it could always rely in the past. The time had come for it to make some concession. Agreement to take part in an Executive before the ending of internment was something, but it did not cut all that much ice with the Unionists who reflected that, if the terrorists were let out, the first people to be shot would probably be members of the SDLP. What was now required was some more positive gesture of modesty. Willingness to allow the Unionists to have the majority in the Executive to which the strength of Unionist feeling in the country (if not the actual representation of Faulknerites in the Assembly) clearly entitled them was a *sine qua non* even of Faulkner's agreement. What was much more important, however, was that the SDLP should now make it clear that it was not trying to manœuvre Ulster into a united Ireland. To do this, it must rest content with a purely inter-governmental and consultative Council of Ireland which was all that the Unionists would buy. By contrast, the SDLP would not budge an inch from its demands. Fortified by the belief that it had the ultimate support of the British Government, it was not even persuaded to call off the rent-and-rates strike until after it had been admitted to the Executive. This stubborn insensitivity may well be seen by posterity as a cruel betrayal of the Catholic population of Ulster, for it was, in the end, responsible for a Protestant reaction which may eventually prove to have put paid to all the aspirations, reasonable and unreasonable, of the Catholic community. Catholics have had to pay heavily for this luxuriant display of SDLP integrity.

On 31 July 1973 the new Assembly met, its proceedings ending in disorder. It was already clear that its twenty-eight unpledged Unionist and 'loyalist' members were attending it mainly for the purpose of disruption—the stated intention of many of them. Against this inauspicious background, Mr Faulkner embarked with the SDLP and Alliance leaders on the task of trying to form an Executive which would satisfy Mr Whitelaw's requirements; Mr Whitelaw was ready to hand to assist in smoothing out all difficulties. One question which a negotiator must always consider is what his 'fall-back' position is going to be. Mr Faulkner had to envisage the possibility that no saleable agreement with the SDLP would prove feasible, in which event the entire British initiative would collapse. In the past, the position of Unionists on this point, including that of Mr Faulkner himself, had always been that if acceptable arrangements for devolved government could not be reached, Unionists would opt for straightforward integration in the United Kingdom, including proper representation at Westminster. As a last resort this policy had much to commend it. It was in line with the pure original doctrine of Unionists and there was evidence that it had much support among Catholic and Protestant opinion. Although British Governments had no zeal for it (particularly Labour Governments which feared increased Unionist representation at Westminster), it was a demand which Britain would find it hard to produce a respectable reason for refusing. In some ways, it was the cleanest possible solution. In Mr Faulkner's eyes, however, it had the disadvantage of having come to be adopted by Dr Paisley.

Total integration, in reality, had no very strong appeal to any Northern Irish politician. Those who wished to take an active part in politics, whatever their party might be, would find their opportunities restricted if there was to be no Northern Irish parliament or Provincial Assembly. There were some signs that Dr Paisley was moving rapidly away from integration and towards the demand, already strongly expressed by Mr Craig, for yet more devolution than there had ever been before. There were a few signs, indeed, that the entire 'loyalist' political movement was drifting in the direction of a plea for a wholly independent Ulster. As for the SDLP, integration was objectionable to it on the ground that it would close the door to Irish unity. Here, then, was a threat which would be applied to all intransigent negotiators—a possible last-resort policy which would have the merit of probably being saleable to the Irish people but distasteful to almost all Northern Irish politicians.

In mid-September, Mr Heath visited Dublin for the purpose of putting pressure on Mr Cosgrave to induce the SDLP to be reasonable. In the course of a television interview, after long and exhausting negotiations, Mr Heath was asked what would happen if agreement could not be reached in Northern Ireland. Off the cuff, he replied that he would think that the right answer would be integration. The history of Mr Heath's personal interventions in the politics of Ulster has on the whole been an unhappy one. His temperament is that of an intensely practical man and therefore far from congenial to the Northern Irish character. On this occasion, either by accident or by instinct, he had made an extremely shrewd move. Naturally, this spread consternation among all parties in Belfast. Mr Faulkner, who should have welcomed it as an effective means of putting pressure on his fellow negotiators, saw it only as a weak-minded concession to Paisleyism. Mr Whitelaw, who should have rejoiced at being presented with a credible and relatively humane ultimate deterrent, was thrown into extreme confusion. The British Prime Minister felt obliged to eat his words publicly (in a letter to the Leader of the Opposition on 19 September 1973) and to make it clear in effect that Britian would never contemplate integration.

This sad little incident had a twofold effect on the Belfast talks and the subsequent Sunningdale negotiations. Mr Faulkner went to the conference table with no fall-back position, a fact which became pathetically evident as the months went on; both the SDLP and the 'loyalists' had been given yet another example of the instability of British policy; and everybody felt that there was much to be said for pressing the British Government as hard as possible. Mr Faulkner, however, had now become too much identified with British policy and too isolated from Unionist opinion in the country to be able to press his own case with any vigour.

What he still retained was a remarkable gift for party management. That was displayed when, on 23 October, he succeeded in carrying with him the Standing Committee of the Unionist Council (the Executive Committee of the party) over the question of participation in a power-sharing Executive. His success in this was staggering proof of the confidence which years of skilful and faithful service had won him, and which months of political error had not squandered. On 22 November, Mr Whitelaw was able to announce in the Commons the formation of an Executive designate to which he would be willing, if it chose to be properly born, to devolve power. Mr Faulkner was given his majority among senior Executive members of which there were to be six Unionists, four members of SDLP and one Alliance member. For this concession, however, the SDLP was to be compensated by two under-secretaryships, and a third was to go to Alliance. By this means, the Unionist demand for an Executive majority was reconciled with the SDLP demand for equal representation in the administration. It was a modest victory for Mr Faulkner. At what cost had it been bought?

The Executive thus happily constructed would not assume office unless and until agreement was reached about those 'all-Irish' institutions which were to be part of the bargain. All that the Unionists were so far committed to was an inter-governmental and consultative Council of Ireland, and the SDLP, with continuing encouragement from Dublin, wanted much more. In the horse-trading which had preceded the formation of the Executive designate, two matters were chiefly at issue: these were the distribution of offices in the projected Administration, and the nature and powers of the new Council of Ireland. It was hard to see how Mr Faulkner could compromise on either of these matters without alienating what remained of his support. Unaccountably, however, Mr Faulkner seemed much more interested in Unionist representation in the Executive than in the whole question of the Irish dimension. This was essentially the reaction of the adept party manager rather than the statesman. Clearly, the Council of Ireland was much the more fundamental and emotive of the two questions. This was to be settled at the conference between representatives of the Northern Irish Executive designate and the British and Dublin Governments at Sunningdale, Berkshire, in December. In reality, however, the broad outlines of the settlement had already been agreed in the talks which had been going on in Belfast. Although there were still complex matters to be settled at Sunningdale, and the conference there rapidly assumed the character so dear to the media of a 'cliff-hanging situation', all the essential terms of the agreement had been settled before the delegates assembled.

In essence, the agreement registered at Sunningdale, after an elaborate and arduous ritual, was this: the British Government would recognize that if ever the people of Northern Ireland freely chose to join a united Ireland, their wishes would not be impeded; the Dublin Government would recognize that Irish unity, if it was to be achieved at all, would be achieved by peaceful means and with the consent of the Northern Irish people. Meanwhile, institutions designed to establish closer co-operation between North and South would be set up. There would be a Council of Ministers which, in the manner of the Council of the European Economic Community, would be able to take decisions only by unanimous vote. This Council would be enabled to acquire Executive functions. Civil servants from North and South would get together to define the various areas— economic, social and cultural—in which the council might suitably act. A secretariat of indeterminate size would be set up to act as agent for the Council of Ireland's decisions. Again in the manner of the EEC, there would be added to the Council of Ministers a consultative Assembly, drawn equally from representatives of the *Dail* and the Northern Irish Assembly. This body would have no power but it would meet to deliberate and pass resolutions. The two delegations of which it would be composed would each be elected on a basis of proportional representation, so that, in practice, whenever the SDLP and the Southern parties voted together they would command a majority.

A sop was offered to the Unionists in the shape of a promise to restore expeditiously the possibility of transferring internal security in Ulster to the Northern Irish Assembly; but this was completely overshadowed by other provisions of the agreement relating to security. It was agreed that the power for suppressing terrorists throughout Ireland should in future be regarded as of paramount common interest. To this end, the Southern Irish Government would set up a Police Authority to supervise the Garda (the Southern Irish police force), and would consult the Northern Irish Executive when appointing members to the Authority. Northern Ireland would reciprocate by consulting Dublin when suggesting members for the Northern Irish Police Authority.

The crucial question of whether the Republic would in fact continue to be a haven for fleeing terrorists from the North proved intractable and was submitted to a Commission of lawyers. This Commission was instructed to consider three possibilities. The only one attractive to the Unionists was that the Southern Irish Government should extend its extradition treaty to cover so-called political offences such as IRA murders of women and children. It was equally clear, however, that this would not be acceptable to the Republic. What it favoured was an advance towards the recognition of Irish sovereignty by the establishment of an all-Irish court. The last possibility (and the one which was destined to be eventually agreed) was a cumbrous system of doubtful value which would enable crimes committed in the North to be tried in the South, and vice versa.

Examined rationally and calmly, the Sunningdale agreement might be seen to inflict no irreparable sacrifices on the Unionists. To begin with, if agreement were not reached on the question of extradition or its alternatives, Sunningdale might never be ratified at all. In the second place, when the civil servants had done their work, they might find that apart from co-operation in the production of tourist brochures there was no suitable area for executive action by the Council of Ireland. Any powers which that body got would in any case have to be given by the Northern Irish Executive. As for the consultative all-Irish

Assembly, that, if it ever got off the ground, could be trusted to become a joke.

Looked at with Unionist eyes, however, the agreement was an unspeakable betrayal. It had created the shell of an all Irish state: it had produced an embryo all-Irish Government in the shape of the Council of Ministers, an embryo all-Irish parliament in the shape of the consultative Assembly, and at least the suggestion of an all-Irish judicature. It had even admitted the Republic to a say in the running of the Ulster police.

Even moderate Unionist opinion was inclined to the view that Mr Faulkner had led Protestant Ulster up the garden path. Was it for this that Unionists had been asked to stomach one humiliation after another and to grant one concession after another? On 4 January 1974, a full meeting of the Unionist Council registered its horror. Shortly afterwards, Mr Faulkner resigned from the party leadership to be succeeded by Mr Harry West. The Assembly Unionists remained as they were and Mr Faulkner continued at their head, but they no longer spoke with the authority of the official Unionists: the supreme organ of the party in the Province had disowned him.

Yet there was another side to this gloomy picture. A power-sharing Executive was actually in operation. A comprehensive agreement between some Protestant politicians on the one hand and the SDLP and Dublin on the other had been made. Mr White-law, the architect of the settlement (who had been translated to higher political service in Britain just before the Sunningdale conference assembled) was being acclaimed as a genius of recon-ciliation by his fellow countrymen. What he had achieved, in harsh reality, was an agreement with Unionist politicians who, by virtue of signing it, had rendered themselves wholly un-representative of any substantial section of Northern Irish opinion. Unwittingly, he had administered a death blow to Mr Faulkner, the only man who might conceivably have sold some sort of power-sharing to Ulster.

Nevertheless, there still seemed to be some hope. A tactful renegotiation of Sunningdale still seemed possible, and the Executive might achieve some practical success. An attenuated Sunningdale might conceivably be sold to the Northern Irish majority if it were represented as an unpleasant but necessary compromise. Such a line, however, was not temperamentally possible for Mr Faulkner. Resilient, courageous, bright-eyed and bushy-tailed as ever, he peddled his Sunningdale wares as the buy of the century. The effect on his supporters was profoundly dispiriting. Given time, he was shrewd enough possibly to repent and to amend this error of presentation; but time was precisely what was denied to him, not on this occasion by a massacre staged by the IRA, but by one of the hazards of British politics, a snap general election for Westminster.

Chapter 10

Total disintegration

One of the cardinal assumptions on which British policy in Ulster was based was that 'the Protestant backlash' was a mere myth. It is not hard to see how this assumption arose. For years it had been one of the chief themes of Nationalist and Republican propaganda.

The Ulster Protestant, it was said, had never really had to fight for his rights. Before the 1914 war, and again immediately after it, the threat of an Ulster rebellion had sufficed to warn the British off any attempt to impose Irish Home Rule. By nature, the Ulster Protestant was loyal and disciplined; the Fenian, on the other hand, was a natural rebel—a contrast, in Republican eyes, highly favourable to the Fenian. It would run counter to Protestant instincts to engage in any kind of guerilla warfare, or to come into open conflict with the forces of the Crown. The tragedy of Britain's policy in Ireland had been the unwillingness of the British ever to call Ulster's martial bluff.

This view of the Protestant psychology seemed to be supported by events. Ulster 'loyalists' had shown zeal enough for street fighting against unarmed students from the Civil Rights Movement in 1968 and 1969, and there had been the few isolated incidents of bombing in early 1970, designed to bring O'Neill down by suggesting that the IRA was still active. As soon as serious IRA warfare had begun in Ulster, however, the Protestants had begun to show astonishing restraint. Even their para-military movements had, on the whole, been remarkably disciplined. Sectarian murders were a relatively late development. What other people would have endured bombing attacks as sustained as those conducted by the IRA since 1970 with so much stolid fortitude? What other people, under terrorist attack, would have shown so much forbearance towards rulers who had actually negotiated with the terrorists? One of the most remarkable features of the Ulster story since 1969 had been the almost mathematically-precise relationship between the growth of Protestant para-military movements and the various vicissitudes of British policy. When the British had gone in for appeasing Republicans, the Protestant barricades had gone up; when the British showed firmness towards Republicans, the Protestant barricades were voluntarily removed. There had, of course, been numerous clashes between the Army and Protestant mobs in the course of which the Army had learnt to respect the courage and physical vigour of Protestant militants, but the Army had always observed the deep embarrassment which these conflicts caused, even to the UDA street leaders. It was hardly surprising, therefore, that the constant stream of advice from British civil servants resident in Belfast, based on what they had been told by the SDLP about the emptiness of Protestant threats, convinced the British Government. It was not until 1974 that the British learnt that they had mistaken discipline and restraint for weakness, that the Protestant community had a degree of internal cohesion and organization which they had never suspected, and that it was in the power of that community, at any moment, to shatter the whole of British policy in Ulster.

It was true that the 'loyalists' were on the whole less adept than the IRA at planting bombs, that their taste ran traditionally to shooting and ferocious unarmed combat, and that this form of warfare was more easily vulnerable to the sheer weight of military superiority than were the underground activities of the IRA. It was also true that, until the later stages of the campaign, Protestants did not have the easy access to sophisticated weaponry which the IRA enjoyed as a result of the support of Iron Curtain, Middle and Far Eastern countries. They did not have either the overwhelming financial support available to the IRA from America, or a secure line of supply and retreat to the Irish Republic. The Protestant armoury, however, although it consisted largely of shotguns, was formidable.

Vastly more important than this (though totally ignored by the British Government) was the vast industrial strength of the Protestant working class. This had only so far been seen in operation in temporary symbolic strikes, such as that which followed the announcement of direct rule. The truth was that a sustained Protestant strike could have paralysed the life of the Province at any moment. All that was awaited was the signal for such a strike, and that would come when the Protestant community had reached the conclusion that Britain was bent on a sell-out. By May 1974 that conviction had been reached. Sunningdale was undoubtedly the crucial turning-point in the slow process of Protestant thought. An intolerable settlement had been imposed by the British Government by guile. A puppet Assembly had been conjured into being in order to sanctify and enforce that settlement. The British had left open no means of constitutional protest against these arrangements, since the Assembly, with what was regarded as its artificially created majority, could remain in being for four years, during which it would have laid the foundations of a united Ireland: so it appeared to an ever-increasing number of Protestants. When, in February, Mr Heath's general election gave that feeling the means of decisive expression, the last objection to direct Protestant action had gone.

One of the favourite criticisms of Mr Heath had always been that he regarded Ulster as a peripheral issue. Rightly or wrongly, the view widely attributed to him was that this Province must not be allowed to become a serious diversion from the grand themes of British policy such as the unification of Europe and the conquest of obstructive trade unionism. Whatever the truth of this criticism, it was hardly likely that any British Prime Minister confronted with the dramatic political crisis which faced Mr Heath at the beginning of 1974 (the miners' strike and the introduction of the three-day week) would allow consideration for Ulster to prevent him from calling a general election which, however misguidedly, he thought was both necessary and likely to give him victory. The fact was, however, that Mr Heath's decision to dissolve was the death warrant of the power-sharing Executive in Ulster and with it the whole of the Heath Government's Ulster policy. Whatever merits the power-sharing experiment might have, it had not been going on long enough to display them. There had been no chance to whittle down the Sunningdale agreement to proportions which might render it palatable to the Northern Irish majority. Mr Faulkner had just lost control of the official Unionist organization and had nothing resembling an efficient election machine at his disposal. His chances of survival, and with them the Executive's chances, depended entirely on avoiding any sort of test of public opinion in Ulster for as long as possible.

Mr Faulkner might conceivably have spared himself and his party the utter humiliation which now followed by remaining as much aloof as possible from the Westminster contest. Because of the curious constitution of the Ulster Unionist party, this course would have been technically open to him. In strict theory, the Unionist Associations in the Province for the purposes of Westminster elections (known locally as 'Imperial elections') are entirely independent of Ulster Unionist headquarters in Belfast and of the local Parliamentary or Assembly party. They are affiliated directly to the National Union of Conservative and Unionist Associations in Britain. To all intents and purposes, Unionist candidates for Westminster seats in Ulster have always been Tory candidates with the single difference that the Conservative party in Britain does not attempt to take any part in their selection and accepts no responsibility for financing them. An Ulster Unionist candidate, therefore, has a direct and exclusive relationship with his constituency Association.

After the removal of Mr Faulkner from the leadership of the official Unionist party, that party formed a coalition with Paisley's Democratic Unionist party and Craig's Vanguard Unionist Progressive party. This coalition was to fight the election on a simple anti-Sunningdale platform. It would have at its disposal the riches and highly developed publicity machine of Paisley's Free Presbyterian Church, the well-organized and firmly established Vanguard movement and, now, the respectability of the official Unionist party. There were still plenty of Unionists, however, who, while intensely dissatisfied with Sunningdale, shrank from open confrontation with Britain and felt a deep distaste for the demagogy of Paisley and Craig. Several of the Imperial Associations chose candidates opposed to the new 'Loyalist' coalition. These candidates were promptly classified by the press as Faulknerites, although many of them had the gravest reservations about Faulkner's acceptance of the Sunningdale agreement. Inevitably, the campaign was fought on a straightforward pro- or anti-Faulkner, pro- or anti-Sunningdale basis. The result exceeded the worst expectations even of Faulkner's most pessimistic supporters: all the candidates to whom he had given his support were slaughtered. Eleven of the twelve Ulster seats at Westminster fell into the hands of the 'Loyalist' coalition, Mr Gerry Fitt succeeding with some difficulty in keeping his majority for the SDLP in West Belfast.

This was, of course, a desperate moral defeat for the Whitelaw settlement. Meanwhile, Mr Heath was also suffering a narrow defeat in Britain. The results of the general election there left the Tories as the strongest single party in the Commons but only barely so. Quite incredibly, some Tories entertained for a while the illusion that the eleven Ulster 'Loyalists' who had just been triumphantly returned in Ulster would tamely agree to sustain a Conservative Government in power; with Liberal support, that would have kept the Tories in office. But the hope was illusory and the Liberal support not forthcoming in any case. Mr Heath accordingly surrendered to Mr Wilson. As far as Ulster was concerned, the election had two consequences: it showed, in the first place, that the power-sharing Executive was governing without consent and, indeed, in the face of the overwhelming hostility of the people of Ulster. It also brought back to power in Britain a party in which Ulster Protestants had even less confidence than they had in the Tory party. Mr Wilson had already publicly committed himself to the view that the ultimate aim of British policy should be the unification of Ireland; he was the first leading British politician to talk to the Provisional IRA and he was subject to constant pressure from a section of his own party which was strongly Irish Republican in its sympathy. Surely, it seemed to those Ulstermen who put the preservation of the Union first, the crunch had come.

In a last minute effort to avert total catastrophe, Mr Faulkner's advisers pressed him to embark on the task of taking the sting out of the Sunningdale agreement: there was still plenty of scope for manœuvre in that respect. It was clear that the Government of the Republic was not going to extend the extradition treaty to cover political offences, and that it would offer nothing beyond the compromise plan for trying offences in the territory where the accused was arrested. This would be a special justification for refusing to implement the plans for a Council of Ireland with executive powers and for a consultative Irish Assembly until the Northern Irish electorate had specifically consented to it. The new Northern Irish Secretary of State, Mr Merlyn Rees (a quietly spoken Welshman of moderate views), was strongly urged to use all the influence he had to secure this postponement. His reaction at first was unfavourable: like other British politicians, he still cherished the hope that Ulster could be hustled into accepting what she was resolved to reject. Mr Faulkner's own Assembly party backbenchers also took a hand: they pleaded with him to secure the removal of the most offensive aspects of Sunningdale before it was too late, to make some concession which would stem the rising tide of Protestant anger. He had to contend, however, with the obdurate resistance of the SDLP and the Dublin Government, with their refusal to sacrifice an ounce of the paper victory they had won.

On 14 May 1974, a 'Loyalist' motion demanding the rejection of Sunningdale was debated in the Assembly and duly and predictably defeated by the Executive's majority. That was the signal for the first clear, organized assertion of Protestant power in Ulster. As soon as the vote was over, the Ulster Workers' Council, a body which virtually no one in Britain had heard of, announced that power cuts would be brought into operation in protest. This was the first act in a Province-wide strike which, in a fortnight, compassed the destruction of the Executive and of the Whitelaw settlement.

This is not the place to describe or to analyse in detail the progress of what must rank as one of the most successful examples of relatively passive resistance on record. The event of the fortnight between 14 May and 29 May ought indeed to be the subject of detailed examination, and perhaps that study ought not to be too long postponed. Here was an instance of a working-class movement which had resolved to achieve a political objective by means of a general strike, precisely the kind of challenge which Mr Heath might have had to encounter in Britain had he been returned to power. In 1926, Britain had successfully resisted a general strike by mustering the voluntary aid of all those in the middle classes and elsewhere who did not share the strikers' objectives. Since then, technological developments are said to have put the country largely at the mercy of a handful of specialist workers without whose co-operation such essentials as electricity supply cannot be maintained. On the face of it, the experience of Ulster during that desperate fortnight seems to justify that view. Other factors were present in Ulster, however, which would not operate in Britain. The Army was already engaged in a law-keeping operation which taxed its powers to the maximum. It could not easily be asked to undertake at the same time the task of running the Province's economy, of manning petrol and power stations. As for voluntary aid in defeating the strike, whence would it be forthcoming?

It was clear that the authorities had made absolutely no provision for the contingencies which now arose. For a week the crisis was allowed to develop with no response from the British Government but strong words about the impropriety of dealing with those who sought to subvert the constitution by industrial action. The incredible hope seems to have lingered that the whole affair would peter out. On the contrary, it rapidly developed, soon encouraged by the strikers' discovery that the State was prepared to subsidize them by the generous provision of supplementary benefit. On May 21 the ludicrous step was taken of despatching Mr Len Murray, General Secretary of the Trades Union Congress, to Belfast to lead a 'back to work' march. This sparsely attended demonstration, which had to be heavily protected by the police and the Army, aroused nothing but contempt and derision. The notion that the Protestant working class of Ulster would instantly respond to the leadership of the head of the British Trade Union movement was seen only as yet another example of the truth that British politicians lacked the remotest idea of what Ulster was about. The next gesture was an ominous announcement by Mr Wilson that the British Government would not for the moment give a further five million pounds to the Harland and Wolff shipyards. The belief that this would bring the strikers to their knees also proved false. Meanwhile, SDLP members of the Executive screamed for decisive action against the strike. It was announced that Mr Wilson would address the nation on the subject by television on 25 May, and it was generally supposed that this would coincide with an instruction to the Army to take over the essential services in Ulster. In the event, the speech was a vigorous denunciation of the strikers, including a calculated insult to massive sections of the Protestant population, who by implication were described as 'spongers' on the British tax-payer. Since the speech was accompanied by absolutely no new action for the next forty-eight hours, it had the effect of arousing contempt as well as indignation. Once again the British Government appeared unworthy both of the trust of its friends and the fear of its enemies.

By 29 May all was over. Mr Faulkner and most of his colleagues in the Executive realized that it was no longer possible to maintain even a semblance of administration without the assent of the strikers. Since Mr Rees would not agree to negotiate with them without abandoning the Government's position that it would not talk to those who sought political objects by industrial action, the Executive had to be written off.

There was much talk in Dublin and among the SDLP about how the British had surrendered pusillanimously to the Protestants and how a Labour Government had knuckled under to the advice of an army which was fundamentally pro-Protestant: neither of these charges holds water. There is ample evidence that the Army carried out promptly every instruction it received, including those which it believed to be beyond its physical power to carry out efficiently. Moreover, it comes ill from those who have continually pointed out the impossibility of suppressing the Catholic population by force to complain of the Government's refusal to go into open combat against what had now become a Province-wide Protestant protest. By the beginning of the second week of the strike, support for it had spread throughout all classes of the Protestant community. Bank managers and suburban golf club secretaries cheered the strikers on. The atmosphere recalled that of Britain in 1940. Although the strike was undoubtedly sustained in its first phases by intimidation, intimidation soon became unnecessary. The whole operation was conducted (with a few exceptions of which the worst was the murder of two Catholics in Antrim during a drunken brawl) with the utmost discipline and efficiency. The strikers virtually took over the task of government. They enforced a petrol rationing scheme and issued passes to those permitted to go to work. They collected and distributed food, carrying with them the farmers who willingly bore severe financial losses in the process. Their public service announcements were read out on the BBC's Ulster Service each morning. Inevitably, there were instances of brutality, theft and peculation, but the prevailing spirit was one of dignified patriotic protest.

For the British public, the strike took the lid off Ulster politics. For years it had been alternatively bored and entertained by reports of the machinations of Ulster politicians and of the British Government's complex dealings with them. The public knew about Faulkner, Paisley, Craig and Bernadette Devlin. From 1972 onwards some more shadowy figures had started to flit across the television screen—UDA leaders (like Tom Herron) in masks. Everyone knew that there were Protestant paramilitary movements which manned barricades, kept 'romper rooms' for the chastisement of erring supporters, and did the occasional murder. The strike, however, revealed a whole new gallery of Ulstermen—hitherto obscure workers, like Harry Murray, who had suddenly proved themselves capable of masterminding a revolution and administering a country. Moreover, these men did not seem to be particularly fanatical. They were simply in deadly earnest about their resolution in no circumstances to accept a settlement which they believed must eventually deprive them and their children of British citizenship. Having achieved their object, they went promptly and peacefully back to work.

The truth was, of course, that this last or penultimate card (for the last is armed rebellion) had been in the pack all the time. A whole unsuspected world existed beneath the surface of Ulster politics. One of the effects of the strife since 1969 had been to call into being innumerable elementary forms of social organization—citizens' committees, factory cells and the like. This had been going on on the Protestant no less than the Catholic side, and the Protestant community, which lives by a martial myth, was by far the better organized of the two. The upshot of it all, it now seemed, was that Mr Whitelaw might well have spared his breath to cool his porridge. He had, it seemed in retrospect, been dancing with shadows. One whiff of reality was all that was needed to bring the whole constitutional structure to ruins. As an example of what happens when a sophisticated political establishment loses contact with gut politics, nothing could be more instructive than the Ulster 'Loyalist' strike.

What passed unnoticed amid all this was the final irony: on 22 May, in the middle of the strike, the Faulkner Executive announced that amendment of Sunningdale which a few weeks earlier might have postponed or even conceivably prevented the strike. Mr Faulkner had been diligently seeking to bring this about since shortly after the February general election. Even Mr Rees had become converted to the idea about a fortnight before the strike began. The Dublin Government was also moving in the right direction, but one citadel remained to be conquered—the SDLP. It was not until after the strike began and as a result of much skilful arm-twisting by Mr Stanley Orme (Minister of State at the Northern Ireland Office and a man congenial to the Catholic politicians) that the SDLP finally yielded. It agreed that the Council of Ireland was to have no executive powers and that the consultative Assembly was not to come into being unless and until those measures had been approved by the Northern Irish electorate. Coming at this time, of course, the new move appeared merely as a concession to the strikers and another proof that British Governments which would not yield to reason will often grovel to force.

The one fact that was indisputable after the strike was that yet another new phase was to begin in the politics of Ulster. With the Executive gone, the Assembly had to be prorogued and direct rule resumed. However, the air was much clearer. The 'Loyalists', having made their point and vindicated their supremacy, were on the whole extremely content. They felt that no further action was called for in the immediate future. The 'Loyalist' politicians, who had alternately appeared in the roles of 'restraining influence' and zealous champions of the strike, consolidated themselves and issued a new programme demanding substantial devolution for Ulster within the framework of a federal United Kingdom. Not only was Mr Paisley, declared integrationist, prepared to accept this programme, but the party surprisingly acquired a new and formidable adherent in Mr Enoch Powell who, having decided that he would not contest the February elections as a Conservative candidate, was to reappear on the scene as the Ulster Unionist Member of Parliament for South Down after the October election. That general election was another staggering victory for the 'Loyalists' in Ulster, although they suffered one casualty in the shape of Mr Harry West, the leader of the party, who succumbed to a united Catholic vote in Fermanagh and Tyrone. Mr Faulkner busied himself in forming a new party which, in accordance with Protestant convention, was also called the Unionist party although, for purposes of differentiation, the phrase 'of Northern Ireland' was added to the title. He carried a faithful remnant into the new organization, but the impression remained that its support was confined to a relatively small section of the middle class in East Ulster. As for the SDLP, its members retired to their boudoirs, occasionally emerging to complain of the many dangers now encompassing the Catholic community. The Dublin Government could also find no constructive response to the dramatic change in the disposition of power in Ulster.

For his part, Mr Merlyn Rees had to go back to the drawing-board. Wisely, he made no attempt to deny the significance of what had occurred. Instead, he spoke, impressively though inaccurately, about the emergence of a new factor, 'Ulster Nationalism', which must now be taken into account. He announced that direct rule would be maintained until a freshly elected Ulster Convention would, in due course, be summoned to draft its own proposals for the constitution, which would then be considered although not necessarily accepted by the British Government. All the emphasis now was on the need for Ulster to take the initiative in seeking her own salvation. For example, it now began to be coolly pointed out in Whitehall that security in Ulster demanded the existence of a strong local police force, a point which had not appeared with equal force to Mr Callaghan in 1969.

As the year went on, the IRA seemed to be losing ground in the Province. Evidence mounted of its growing unpopularity with the Catholic population; it suffered, as unfortunately many others did also, from the rising spate of Protestant murders. Although the weak policing of Catholic areas placed it largely beyond the reach of the law, internment was taking its toll and, but for the elaborate precautions with which the system was still being operated, and the inadequacy of Northern Ireland's supply of prisons, would have taken a greater toll still. The IRA, however, had another card to play, and this it now produced with astonishing results.

It had been the IRA's strategy to concentrate its attack principally on Ulster. The theory no doubt had been that a concerted attack on Britain might well rally the British people in support of an anti-IRA campaign which, so long as the war was only conducted in Northern Ireland, would seem remote and possibly irrelevant to British interests. On the whole, this policy had paid off. As time went on and casualties and expenditure increased, there was undoubtedly a growing disenchantment in Britain with the 'Ulster entanglement': this was reflected particularly in a powerful 'get-out-of-Ulster' movement in the Labour party. However, the Labour Government, with the support of the Opposition, still seemed a long way from surrendering to this demand. As the IRA military plight grew worse in Ulster and its unpopularity mounted there, there seemed much to be said for switching attention to Britain. At this stage in the game, it was doubtless reasoned, a bombing campaign there would be more likely to strengthen the demand for withdrawal from Ulster than to unite the British people in hostility to the IRA.

Following the bombing outrage at Aldershot in February 1972, no further serious attacks were made in Britain for a year. The Border Poll in Northern Ireland in March 1973 was marked by a series of explosions in central London, including one outside the Courts of the Old Bailey. There followed then a series of intermittent attacks, most of them small by Northern Irish standards, starting at the end of August. Between 18 August 1973, and the end of January 1975, there were 262 explosions in England, including those caused by incendiary devices. The most serious of these was an attack on public houses in Birmingham on 21 November 1974, designed as a protest against the public ban on a funeral procession in Coventry for an IRA man who had killed himself in the process of planting a bomb. The Birmingham explosions caused twenty-one deaths. Their effect on British public opinion was dramatic. Strident demands were made in the House of Commons for the restoration of the death penalty for terrorist offences. Ulstermen did not hesitate to point out the contrast between the response of British opinion to the bombing of Britons and the patience which the British showed when Ulster was the target. Only two years earlier, Parliament had deliberately removed the death penalty for the murder of soldiers and policemen in Ulster (it had remained on the Statute book there, although it had not been used for several years). Although, in the end, the Commons shrank from bringing back the gallows in Britain, the Government was moved to introduce new anti-terrorist legislation specifically aimed against the IRA's British activities.

It was significant, however, that one of the main provisions of this legislation empowered the Home Secretary to return suspected IRA terrorists caught in Britain to Ulster, if that happened to be their normal place of residence. This indeed implied a strange interpretation of the Union. It suggested that Britain regarded Ulster as a suitable dumping-ground for terrorists, and that her chief preoccupation was to set up a *cordon sanitaire* around her own shores. Could it be that the IRA bombings were producing their intended effect by fostering the feeling in Britain that she had been dragged into an alien war which had no bearing on her own interests?

By the end of 1974, events had occurred in Ulster itself which brought the whole nature and purpose of British policy once again into question. Belfast buzzed with rumours, all promptly denied, of new British approaches to the IRA. Then it was revealed that a group of Protestant clergymen (with the knowledge, and some said more than the knowledge, of the British Government) had held exploratory discussions with IRA leaders and reported their conclusions back to Mr Merlyn Rees. There followed the familiar charade. The British Government stuck firmly to the view that it would not negotiate with the IRA. It was perfectly prepared, however, to receive reports from others of the IRA's wishes and to indicate through third parties what its response to hypothetical IRA actions, such as a truce, would be. It was also prepared for its own civil servants in Belfast to enter into discussions with the Provisional *Sinn Fein*, the political wing of the

Provisional IRA (the ban on this organization had been lifted by Mr Merlyn Rees). The fact that it never pretended to be anything but an agent of the IRA and that members of the IRA Command were free, whenever it suited their books, to present themselves to the world as members of the Provisional *Sinn Fein* did not affect the issue.

The upshot of these long-distance communications was a fortnight's truce which was eventually extended indefinitely. Mr Rees publicly committed himself to respond to this gesture by releasing internees and reducing the intensity of security operations. More staggering still, he entered into arrangements for the establishment of 'incident centres' manned by British civil servants and to be paralleled by 'incident centres' set up by the Provisionals. By this means, the two sides would be able to maintain constant communication with each other in the interests of preserving the armistice, although the proprieties were still to be observed by the rule that when British civil servants addressed the IRA they would continue to do so through *Sinn Fein*.

From the IRA's point of view, something very near to a recognition of belligerent status had been achieved. More important still, its 'incident centres' could be developed into IRA police stations. The argument was simple: if the IRA was to enforce the truce on its own supporters (many of whom in Belfast hated it) it must be free to discipline them. By the middle of February the IRA was publicly demanding its own police force in its own areas, and the UDA was responding by declaring its intention to police its own areas; everything pointed to the imminent return of Protestant and Catholic enclaves from which all lawful authority was excluded. It looked as though everything the Army had achieved since the 'Motorman' operation on 31 July 1972 was to be cast away. Meanwhile, both sides continued to murder, the IRA continued to import arms and Mr Rees, in token of his good faith, continued to release detainees, most of whom, on past form, could be assumed to be bent on returning as rapidly as possible to the front line.

The Dublin Government, which had been induced at long last to tackle the problem of punishing IRA fugitives from the North, was again thrown into consternation by the spectacle of Britain doing business with the enemy; the SDLP feared that the British were about to sacrifice them for the sake of a deal with Republican terrorists, and Protestant 'Loyalists' and moderate

Unionists alike discerned more clearly than ever the signs of a British 'sell-out'.

Where, then, will this policy lead? What, then, can now be done to redeem its consequences? And what, if any, wisdom can be rescued from the follies and the crimes which have marked the British role in Ulster since 1969?

Chapter 11

Conclusion

Three distinct and competing themes can be discerned in the gloomy story of British policy in Ulster since 1969. The first, pursued diffidently and intermittently from time to time, may be called 'the theme of legitimacy'. The theory which was originally invoked to justify the despatch of troops to Ulster was the simple one that lawful institutions in a part of the United Kingdom were being threatened by violence and that the military should therefore go to the aid of the civil power. From the first, however, that theory lived uneasily alongside a totally different conception of the purpose of what was thought of as 'British intervention'. 'Legitimism' can only be said to have been in the ascendant for a few months during Mr Maudling's tenure of responsibility for Northern Ireland. From 9 August 1971, the date on which internment was reintroduced, until 30 January 1972, the date of 'Bloody Sunday', it appeared that the British Government was genuinely trying to support a Stormont which had given overwhelming evidence of its commitment to reform in the thorough-going enforcement of order.

'Bloody Sunday', however, saw the birth of a new theme or, more precisely, the return, in a much more radical form, to a motif which had been clearly evident under Mr Callaghan. The new phase was that of the 'political initiative'. So long as it lasted, the chief aim of British policy was the creation of some sort of coalition of the 'centre' in Northern Irish politics which, in a trite and fashionable phrase, would 'bridge the gulf between the communities'. The negative purpose was to destroy the unity of the monolithic Unionist party, though this was still under strongly liberal leadership. Out of the wreckage it was hoped to build up some sort of Protestant political movement thoroughly acceptable to British taste and willing to collaborate with moderate Catholic politicians against all manner of extremists. This, it was argued, would give the security forces the popular backing they needed for victory.

This policy in turn failed for reasons which are transparently clear: any coalition between Catholics and Protestants must rest on the willingness of each side to abandon, if only temporarily, any position which was wholly unacceptable to the other. A prudent (one is tempted to say a sane) British Government would have asked at the outset what scope existed for such compromise, and the answer should have been obvious to anyone of normal political intelligence. What the Protestant community was resolved on above all else was that it should not be nudged or manœuvred, let alone coerced, into a united Ireland. No settlement involving anything which looked remotely like a step in that direction would be acceptable to it. The Catholic SDLP, on the other hand, had two clear demands: one was for an assured place, not just for Catholics but for Catholics who were committed to Irish unity on a Republican basis, in executive government. The other was for the creation of institutions which would materially advance the cause of Irish unity.

It was just conceivable that the first of these objects—executive power-sharing—could be achieved if the second were abandoned. If, at any moment, the SDLP had declared convincingly that it would renounce the desire for immediate all-Irish institutions and confined itself to the peaceful advocacy of Irish unity at general elections, an agreement between it and the Unionists just might have been reached. So long as all-Irish institutions of an apparently powerful kind remained one of the immediate objects of the SDLP, however, no Unionist of whatever temperature would be happy about admitting the SDLP to a position in government from which it too might seek to promote the cause of Irish unity. If executive power-sharing was to come about, therefore, it must be at the cost of sacrificing the idea of a strong Council of Ireland. This truth was never grasped either by the SDLP or by Mr Whitelaw. The consequence was the Sunningdale agreement, which totally alienated the Protestant community, accomplished the political destruction of Mr Faulkner, and led inevitably to the decisive assertion of Protestant power in the 'Loyalist' strike of 1974.

A no less powerful factor in frustrating phase two of British policy was the failure of the British Government to distinguish between political and social reforms in Northern Ireland which might placate the Catholic community, and concessions in the field of security, such as the release of internees, which could only have the effect of increasing the military potential of the IRA, enhancing its prestige and augmenting its capacity to intimidate. The proper basis for a deal with the SDLP was reasonable political concessions from the Unionist side in return for wholehearted support for the security forces from the SDLP. It is more than likely that no such deal would have been acceptable to the SDLP which throughout preferred the integrity of its principles to the safety and welfare of the Catholic community; but the deal was never attempted, because British politicians never had the sense to see that it was an essential condition of the success of the policy on which they had embarked.

The third discernible theme of British policy was an attempt to do a deal with the men of violence, if necessary sacrificing in the process the men of moderation. The first clear experiment in this direction was Mr Whitelaw's negotiations with the IRA in the summer of 1972. This aberration failed rapidly for one simple reason: the IRA is a fanatical body which believes itself to be already endowed with the moral authority to fulfil the aims of Irish revolution. Its minimum conditions—a declaration of intent to end the Union and withdraw all United Kingdom troops from the North—amount to a demand for unconditional surrender. It will accept no less. If it is beaten, it will prefer, as it did in 1963, quietly to retire from the field; it will never formally concede victory by modifying its claims.

Nevertheless, Mr Whitelaw's experience has not prevented Mr Merlyn Rees from reverting to the fatal experiment of June 1972 and doing so, indeed, in a far more extravagant form. The truce arrangements which the present British Government has made with the IRA put Mr Whitelaw's brief flirtation entirely in the shade. They involve a degree of recognition to the Provisional IRA greater than any which has been thought of hitherto. They threaten the restoration of no-go areas, Catholic and Protestant, and they pose the question as to whether any British Government which had gone thus far can have any other intention than to abandon Ulster to civil war. The war objectives of the IRA, it must be observed, remain unchanged. What changes have there been in the objectives of British policy?

The main criticism of British policy must be that successive governments during the period discussed have never known with anything like clarity which of the three alternative themes described above they were pursuing. They have idly drifted from one to another, and they have failed altogether to differentiate between the respective objectives of these policies or to consider the means by which those objectives were most likely to be achieved. It is tempting to say that in this they have simply displayed the familiar defects of hand-to-mouth, empirical British politics. That, however, is untrue. Mr Whitelaw's qualities, for instance, were not those of the typical *grand seigneur* (lack of imagination compensated for by a firm grasp of day to day realities). Too often, alas, his initiative carried him beyond the limits of the possible and, in a muddled kind of way, he practised a style of rationalistic politics utterly different from the instinctive politics on which his party prides itself. It is a liberal illusion that negotiation is itself a form of therapy which will always prevail over the crude facts of power. Like a true liberal, Mr Whitelaw coupled a failure to recognize the existence of any really obdurate obstacle to a sensible and harmonious settlement, with the liberal's tendency to underrate important but unpalatable facts. That he retained so much popularity in Northern Ireland and elsewhere in spite of this policy is a great tribute to the courtesy and manifest honesty with which he conducted it.

The question remains whether anything tolerable can be rescued from the mess. No one should shrink from prophecy about Northern Ireland. The most remarkable feature of events there since 1969 has been their predictability. Critics of the British handling of this affair are not open to the accusation that they are showing hindsight. Most of them may claim to have foreseen well in advance every successive disaster.

The question which those critics must now consider, however, is whether, by one of those miraculous dispensations which are sent to save British politicians from themselves, the three conflicting policies which have been pursued since 1969 are about to converge in a synthesis which could even produce something like 'a solution' for the Northern Irish problem.

This is in fact the claim which is now being made for what appears on the surface to be the strange conduct of Mr Merlyn Rees since December 1974. The argument, although it is seldom fully articulated, runs thus: Mr Rees has gone further than any of his predecessors towards making a formal agreement with the IRA. This agreement carries with it grievous dangers, but it also contains certain hopeful potentialities. The danger is obviously that the IRA will use an armistice to strengthen its position and to re-establish Republican no-go areas and that this will provoke similar measures from the Protestant para-military formations. It will also, however, have certain other consequences. It will frighten the SDLP and all moderate official Unionists by giving them the impression that Britain is about to abandon Ulster to the extremists from both camps and to sell out the blessed 'centre'. Terrified by this prospect, Alliance men (for what they may be worth), Faulknerite Unionists, and even the more responsible elements of the 'Loyalist' coalition (particularly the Official Unionists), will begin to show an unaccustomed disposition to sink their differences and club together. For its part the Northern Irish electorate, both grateful for the cessation of hostilities and worried by the prospect of a British sell-out to extremists, will return more moderate men to the Convention than was hitherto thought possible. Paradoxically, the result of Britain's latest flirtation with the IRA will turn out to be the constitution of an effective Northern Irish 'centre' at long last. The outward tokens of this will be agreement on some mode of power-sharing, though probably not precisely that which was embodied in the 1973 Act. Just as important, it will also be agreement by the SDLP to back a possibly reorganized police force and to urge Catholics to join it. This happy outcome will enable the full force of the Northern Irish community to be mobilized equally against Republican and any surviving Protestant militants.

By the time this book is published, it may be possible to judge whether this sanguine prophecy (now made by some of Mr Rees's apologists) is showing signs of becoming true. It would be cowardly, therefore, for me to shrink from laying on record my belief that it will not. The main objection to this happy prognosis is that if it shows the smallest sign of being realized, all the forces of militant Republicanism and militant Protestantism will be summoned into action to frustrate it. It is hard to see how it could be realized without a reasonably prolonged truce, and the signs are that the existing truce (April 1975) is cracking. Evidence mounts that the Provisional IRA is preparing, by arms imports and by re-training, to resume its campaign; there seems little doubt that its Belfast Brigade would already have opened hostilities again but for the restraint urged upon it by the Provisional Army council in Dublin. Meanwhile, bitter internecine quarrels have broken out within the Republican movement and free-lance murder by Catholics and Protestants continues to flourish. When, added to all this, there are the provocations inevitably associated with the activity of any deliberative assembly in Northern Ireland, the chances of maintaining an armistice seem slim. Once the armistice has ended, what reason is there for supposing that the familiar tendency for the community to polarize in response to the conflict between extremists will not appear again?

Even if this gloomy though probable hypothesis is rejected, the question will still remain—what conceivable constitutional compromise will the Convention, left to its own devices, be able to work out as a whole for the hoped-for coalescence of moderate forces? It seems certain that the 1973 Constitution now commands very little, if any, support in Northern Ireland. The various alternatives sketched in an illuminating Green Paper by the British Government, which draws edifying examples from the experience of distant countries faced with the problems of the multi-national state, do not seem to arouse much enthusiasm either. The solid facts that remain are the apparently irrevocable commitment of the SDLP to executive power-sharing and the equally irrevocable commitment of the 'Loyalist' and Unionist majority to majority rule based on party government and collective cabinet responsibility. The clash between these irreconcilable formulae spells deadlock. The faith on which British policy has rested, that logically incompatible objects can be reconciled simply by submitting them to the healthy process of negotiation, has so far not been justified.

It seems highly likely, therefore, that before many months are out the British Government will be forced to do what it has hitherto stubbornly refused to do—to ask the fundamental questions presented by its relationship with Ulster. Curiously enough, the asking and answering of those questions have been inhibited by the persistence of the view that one of the options facing British policy is that of deliberately promoting the unification of Ireland. Wide-ranging discussions of the future of Ulster tend always to get bogged down in speculation on a highly metaphysical question—whether Ireland is or is not a nation. Subconsciously, most Englishmen probably assume that the answer is that Ireland is a nation or, if she is not, that she certainly ought to be one. As Mr Powell has pointed out, the fact that the Irish of North and South occupy the same island is no more proof that they share a common nationhood than the fact that the Spanish and Portuguese share the same peninsula proves that they constitute a nation. What does stand out is that the

Protestant Irish who occupy the north-east of Ireland are utterly resolved not to form a common political unit with the Irish of the Republic. Nationhood does not necessarily express itself in a demand for separate and sovereign political institutions; whether two bodies of people, one of which is absolutely resolved to form no such common unit with the other, can be said to constitute a nation is a matter of semantics which has little to do with political reality. The principle which Britain has traditionally espoused, in any case, is not that nations must be forced to express their nationhood in common political institutions, but that, where practicable, those who wish to form such institutions should be enabled to do so. This is what is meant by 'self-determination'. No one denies that Protestant Ulstermen have much in common with Catholic Southern Irishmen. Ulster Unionism, for instance, owes its *raison d'être* to Irish Republicanism, and Irish Republicans would have little to live for now if the disappearance of Ulster Unionism were to deprive them of their chief object of hatred. The histories of Ulster and the Republic are inextricably intertwined, but so is the history of Britain with that of Ireland as a whole. Economically also, both parts of Ireland are more dependent on the British mainland than they are upon each other.

The problem would obviously be simpler if the form which the political aspirations of Ulster Protestants took was a demand for independence. So far, however, this has not been the case. What is lately become fashionable to call 'Ulster nationalism' still mainly expresses itself in a passionate demand for continued incorporation in the United Kingdom. Can this demand be justly denied?

The disadvantages of the Ulster connection to Britain are now almost too obvious to need listing. Although Ulster's contribution to the British Exchequer has always been underrated, there can be no doubt that, even in normal conditions of peace, Ulster imposes a heavy burden on the British taxpayer comparable with that imposed by many other parts of the United Kingdom which draw from the public purse more than they put into it. Added to this, Ulster saddles Britain with a perennial 'minority problem' with which she has often proved to be extremely ill-equipped to deal. Since 1969 that problem has involved Britain in a vast military commitment and a steadily mounting annual cost (see Appendix IV). Moreover, as the Ulster battle has spread to the mainland it has exposed the British people themselves to physical attack. In the past even these disadvantages would have seemed a small price to pay for a British foothold in Ireland, the strategic importance of which in time of war had been repeatedly proven. Britain, however, no longer thinks in traditional strategic terms. It is doubtful indeed whether she now thinks in terms of defence at all. This factor removed, the argument, from the standpoint of British interests, for a straightforward abandonment of Ulster seems highly cogent.

It is, however, a false and thoroughly unrealistic argument. In terms of *realpolitik* there might have been something to be said for it in 1969. To spend five years in an effort to suppress guerilla warfare in a part of the United Kingdom and then simply to admit defeat would obviously now be a direct invitation to subversion in the rest of the United Kingdom. The instant withdrawal of British troops, furthermore, would plunge the whole of Ireland into anarchy on a scale hitherto unimagined. Whatever side emerged victorious would almost certainly be anti-British and would tend to look for support to Britain's enemies. Already both the IRA and some of the Protestant para-military movements receive substantial aid from such quarters as central Europe and the Middle East. Even if traditional strategy is out of date, British security is hardly compatible with the existence of a Cuba a few miles from her Western shores. Any notion that the vacuum created by the withdrawal of United Kingdom troops would be promptly and smoothly filled by a successful invasion of the North by the Irish Republic and, as a result, the establishment throughout Ireland of a peaceful, if rather inefficient and corrupt *bourgeois* state, is absurd. It exaggerates both the capacity and the will of the Southern Irish to undertake the daunting task of governing Ulster.

In moral terms, straightforward withdrawal or refusal to get involved might have been tolerable in 1969. Left to themselves the Unionists of the North might well have suppressed the revolution in its first phases. The operation might have been somewhat rougher than the British would have liked, but it would not necessarily have been incompatible with a more or less liberal regime at Stormont which could eventually have resumed the operation of seeking to reconcile the Catholic population by reform. What happened, on the contrary, was that Britain came onto the scene in force, deprived the Ulster majority, by disarming the police and disbanding the B-Specials, of the means of self-defence, and encouraged the rebels by gratifying their demands. To follow all this, after five years of misery and bloodshed, by simply abandoning the people of Ulster to their own fate would be the most discreditable act in recorded British history.

All this is indeed half consciously perceived by British politicians. They know, without being able to say precisely why, that it is impossible simply to get out of Ulster. Any withdrawal must therefore be preceded by some settlement which at least fraudulently purports to have established the framework of a stable government. What is more, any such settlement must at least appear to be consistent with the discharge of Britain's much vaunted commitments to the Catholic minority.

In practice, all this would mean the following things: United Kingdom forces would have to remain in large enough numbers to ensure the preservation of order until adequate local means for enforcing security had been set up. The Ulster Defence Regiment might be turned over to the control of a new Ulster state, but the police would also have to be strengthened and made as acceptable as possible to the population. Since, if executive power-sharing is unacceptable in the framework of the United Kingdom and under the guarantee of the Westminster Parliament, it will certainly not be acceptable in an independent Ulster, some alternative means of safeguarding the Catholic community would have to be found. The need for safeguarding that community and the difficulty in doing so have both been gratuitously increased by the failures of British policy. Unionism is no longer liberal; a Protestant population, enraged by years of suffering at the hands of the IRA, is bent on crushing the enemy once and for all and sees the enemy, to an ever-increasing extent, as the entire Catholic community. The Catholic community, for its part, has been encouraged to develop pretensions far more ambitious than it has ever had before.

Obviously, the only foundation for a settlement based on independence would be an attempt to separate the Protestant and Catholic communities. It would certainly be possible to redraw the boundary in such a manner as to detach certain predominantly Catholic areas in the West from Ulster and incorporate them in the Republic. This would involve saddling the Republic with an unwanted, turbulent and often poverty-stricken population. It would not please Dublin, but it would be hard for Dublin to find a respectable reason for declining Irish territory and it would certainly be more acceptable to the Republic than the creation of a third Irish state in Western Ulster which would stand a fair chance of falling under the domination of the IRA. Any redrawing of the boundary, however, would leave a solid, disaffected and defenceless body of Catholics in the heart of Belfast. The Protestant community would see them as a perpetual threat to its existence and would almost certainly anticipate that threat by violent action. A swift campaign of incendiarism is the form which such action would probably take. The forcible transfer of Belfast Catholics from the North to the Republic would be a physical impossibility. They would not want to go, and it would be extremely hard for the predominantly rural Republic to incorporate this urban and industrial population. The most the British Government could do would be to salve its conscience by offering some sort of bribe for voluntary migration. It would also, no doubt, be called upon to subsidize the Dublin Government to enable it to guarantee British standards of social security to the formerly British citizens which it was being called upon to take in. The cost of the exercise would be substantial.

It is conceivable that the Provisional IRA would accept this 'solution' since it would secure their immediate objective—the ending of the Union—and since it could be represented as a step towards Irish unification. On the other hand, it seems unlikely that most of the Protestant para-military movements would be willing to swallow it. They would object violently to the surrender of territory it involved. The cry 'not an inch' would be heard again. It is more than probable, therefore, that the operation would bring the United Kingdom Army and the British Government into open collision with large sections of the resulting Protestant community. Relations would be likely to be permanently embittered. Above all, however, the realistic objection to this course is that, far from giving immediate relief to the British, it would impose upon them the need, after six years' exhausting struggle, to embark on a new campaign in Ulster. If that exercise were successfully conducted, it is not clear that it would produce anything greatly preferable to what would result from immediate unashamed withdrawal. When the British had gone, the Provos would resume their campaign and the Official IRA might well turn its attention to the task of spreading chaos in the expanded territories of the Republic. Britain would have spent yet more money and blood on a policy designed to give an appearance of respectability to surrender and betrayal. That, however, is not unprecedented in her history.

It is not, unfortunately, to be supposed that this policy, or some civilized version of it, can be altogether ruled out. The stark truth is that if Ulster can be shown to be ungovernable by Britain, Britain will be justified in abandoning the attempt to govern her. What is more, if this truth comes to be widely understood in Ulster, the chances of achieving a settlement within the framework of the Union could well be increased. It is high time that ultimate British withdrawal was frankly recognized as a possibility, not simply invoked as a vague threat or dismissed from the mind as 'unthinkable'. If Britain were eventually to be driven to embark on this horrific course, it would be important for the British public to understand what the policy meant, what its dangers were, and how they could be best and most honourably diminished. It would be important, for instance, for the British Government to adopt a friendly and encouraging attitude towards any kind of independence which might come into being as a consequence of free negotiation. Nothing could be more damaging or ruinous to the interests of the Catholic minority than for the British to treat such a state—the creature, after all, of their own failure—as a monstrosity to be penalized and persecuted. There would be much to be said for generous economic aid to such a state so long as it did not show itself to be bent on oppression. The glib assertion that an independent Ulster would in any case be economically unviable is far from proven. Such a state might derive solid advantages from membership of the Common Market; it is arguable also that it could prosper on a basis of total free trade with the rest of the world. Yet the dangers of this experiment are so monstrous that it cannot be honourably and sanely contemplated, save as a last resort. It is as such, and only as such, that it should now be soberly envisaged.

It is part of the argument of this essay that the chance of keeping Ulster within the United Kingdom on a basis of regional devolution has now been lost. The terms which even the most moderate Catholic politicians have been encouraged to demand as part of such a settlement are manifestly not going to be acceptable to the Protestant majority; the Protestant majority is no longer in any mood to show proper tolerance to the minority. Liberal Unionism has for the moment been extinguished by British folly. The familiar theme that the whole of the United Kingdom is moving towards devolution and that it should be possible to reproduce in Ulster essentially the same kind of settlement as that now being envisaged for Scotland or Wales does not hold water. Neither Scotland nor Wales has a minority problem analogous to that of Ulster. Neither Scotland nor Wales would tolerate the power-sharing arrangements which it has been sought to impose on Ulster. If Ulster is to remain in the United Kingdom, therefore, the conclusion seems logically irresistible that, in respect of all the functions of central government, she must be administered from Whitehall. After all, this was the condition of the whole of Ireland from 1802 to 1922, and during much of that period it proved quite compatible with a high level of administrative efficiency.

Any such arrangement would, of course, involve raising the representation of Ulster at Westminster to a reasonable level. About twenty, as distinct from twelve, seats would be needed to put that representation on a par with that of Scotland. In the form in which it has so far been presented (by politicians such as Dr Paisley and Mr Powell), this policy has had nothing whatsoever to commend it either to the Dublin Government or to the Catholic minority in the North. Under the heading of 'total integration', it has usually appeared as a simplistic solution designed to settle Ulster once and for all by affirming that she is and will remain a part of the United Kingdom. It is usually accomplished by proposals designed to emphasize with equal force that the Republic is a foreign state, the citizens of which should enjoy none of the anomalous privileges which British law still affords them. Thus presented, the policy has acquired an anti-Irish flavour. It has seemed to be designed to block once and for all the aspirations towards Irish unity. Just as the majority of British politicians have tended not to reckon with the Protestant majority in Ulster, so Mr Powell and his like do not reckon with the Catholic minority. They emphatically do not advocate that this minority should be oppressed or that it should have anything but the fullest rights of British citizenship. They can justly affirm that a large section of that minority has habitually been content with membership of the United Kingdom and that much of it feels positive loyalty to the Queen. None of this alters the fact, however, that the aspiration towards Irish unity is and will remain a factor of crucial importance in the politics of Ulster. Many thousands of Ulster Catholics will demand not only the right to campaign peacefully for Irish unity, but also some clear recognition that the British Government does not regard the status of Ulster as necessarily settled for ever; that it acknowledges that if a clear majority of the Province's people ever wants unification on terms compatible with justice for the Protestant minority, Britain will not stand in the way of the realization of that aim.

The best means of embodying that guarantee is the institution of the plebiscite. Periodic plebiscites, however, could be productive of disorder. A far better method would be a continuing plebiscite built into the normal electoral system. If, at every general election, voters were invited not only to indicate the candidate of their choice but also, on a separate ballot paper, to declare whether they favoured unification or the maintenance of the Union, a standing recognition of the right of self-determination would have been provided. In time this could also make for a happy state of affairs in which the dominant factor in Ulster parliamentary elections was no longer the Border. Since the electorate would be able to express its views on that subject by means of a plebiscite, the need to use parliamentary elections as a method of expressing national loyalties would no longer exist. It is at least possible that the very regularity and normality of a built-in plebiscite of this kind would make for stability. There is certainly no reason to believe that it would be an additional source of friction.

Another Catholic aspiration which is partly practical in character is the desire for 'all-Ireland' functional institutions. The arguments for close co-operation in spheres like tourism, power-supply and regional development are extremely strong. In sober moments they have come to be recognized by Unionist politicians. The greatest obstacle to their realization has been the dedicated attempt by the SDLP to represent all such practical proposals as steps towards Irish unity. Under arrangements by which the functions of central government in Ulster were carried out by a Civil Service ultimately responsible to Westminster, the obstacles to this kind of co-operation could be reduced.

None of this would involve subjecting Ulster, without any allowance for local circumstances, to 'British rule'. A Secretary of State for Ulster, who by custom could be an Ulsterman, would preside over various departments of central government in the Province as the Secretary of State for Scotland now presides over the departments of the Scottish government. A junior minister could be more or less permanently resident in Belfast. The Ulster Civil Service would continue to be manned largely by Ulstermen and to function largely from the Province. Separate Ulster legislation would be enacted at Westminster when necessary, as separate Scottish legislation is enacted there now. An Ulster Grand Committee, like the Scottish Grand Committee in the Commons, could be charged with the detailed scrutiny of that legislation. In practice, the Stormont Parliament largely occupied itself during most of its history in re-enacting Westminster statutes. The autonomy enjoyed by Ulster under the old system was in a high degree illusory: the effective influence of local opinion under the system proposed here would be real.

One of the chief obstacles to the administrative efficiency of direct rule was the absence (in practice) throughout the whole period of effective machinery of local as distinct from regional government in the Province. It is ironic (and no great tribute to the foresight of Ulster politicians) that on the very eve of Stormont's destruction, Mr Faulkner's Government adopted the Macrory reforms which vested all the substantial functions of the local authorities in the Stormont Parliament. When that Parliament ceased to operate, these functions fell on the shoulders of the luckless Secretary of State. The Macrory reforms won wider public support even in the Catholic community than anyone would have dared to predict. Although Stormont was a Unionist-dominated Parliament, the minority had come to repose great and justifiable faith in its Civil Service. Had Stormont survived, the case for the Macrory system would have been overwhelming. In the present circumstances, however, one of the chief objects of policy must be to find a way of achieving proper Catholic participation in government without recourse to the impossible expedient of executive power-sharing at a regional level. The most obvious way to do this would be to resuscitate local government, and the demand for this is already very strong in Ulster. It would not be necessary to re-establish a vast number of local authorities. The Province could be divided into three or four large regional areas which would provide the upper layer of a two-tier system of local government. One or possibly two of these regional councils would be under permanent Catholic control. At the lower level of local government, where the politics are those of the parish pump, effective power-sharing between the communities has often proved remarkably easy to achieve.

Such a structure of local government could have an immediate and crucial advantage. The battle against the IRA will not be won, it is now generally agreed, without the aid of a much strengthened and more widely accepted police force. The RUC, demoralized by the Hunt reforms and subjected to constant criticism from

Britain, will never again, in the opinion of some of its most ardent admirers, secure a foothold in the Catholic community. In certain Catholic areas its effectiveness was always small; nevertheless, it was able to maintain the essentials of law and order and to keep track of rebellious elements. It now seems almost indisputable, however, that law enforcement in Ulster calls for a number of local forces which reflect in their composition the predominant character (Protestant or Catholic) of the areas in which they function. In this as in everything else there are desperate dangers. Protestant and Catholic para-military movements will be alert to penetrate such forces. At the very best, it will be almost certainly impossible to reproduce under this system the high quality of RUC recruitment in the past. A relatively inefficient police force, nevertheless, is better than no force at all. In many Catholic areas this is now the choice.

The ultimate responsibility for the reorganization of the police would, under the arrangement sketched here, rest with Westminster. That in itself would be no great source of encouragement to Ulstermen. In the context, however, of full representation at Westminster and of a system which unreservedly committed the British Government to the task of governing Ulster, it could well be acceptable. After all, the RUC and its auxiliaries were creatures of British legislation. As for local police control, the system of local government suggested here would obviously lend itself to that function. Police authorities with a balanced representation of the communities in each area could be subjected to scrutiny by the new local authorities. The result would be something like the British system of watch committees.

This broad settlement offers three positive advantages to the Catholic community and to the Dublin Government. It offers the minority in Northern Ireland a degree of actual participation in government far greater than it could get under any alternative system which is now conceivable; it offers the only recognition of the aspiration towards Irish unity compatible with Britain's obligation to the Protestant majority; and it offers the only prospect now remaining of achieving functional co-operation between North and South. To the Protestant community it offers a far clearer and more permanent British commitment to the defence and government of Ulster than did the Stormont system, and it does not violate the principle of majority rule.

In spite of these admirable qualities, however, the reactions of Northern Irish politicians to these proposals will, in the first instance, undoubtedly be uniformly hostile. This settlement would embody Dr Paisley's original demands (proper representation at Westminster and administrative integration with Britain), although there is strong evidence that he has modified these. There is, however, a limit to the extent to which the British Government should strive to meet his precise requirements. Northern Irish politicians generally could be expected to look askance at a system which reduced personal political advantages in the Province. What is more, the settlement, like all other possibilities, involves real dangers. What if the local councils became enclaves of factional power? What if Catholic-dominated councils again raised the tricolour and sent their minutes to Dublin? What if the local police forces became 'sectarian armies'? None of these possibilities can be wholly discounted. The answer is that at least a loyal and powerful Civil Service would be there to anticipate and guard against these possibilities. A council which started to exceed its powers could be subdued by the method familiar in Irish history and only recently applied in Londonderry. Its functions could be temporarily vested in an unelected commission of reliable local notables. The possibilities of disintegration would be far less than they would be if the alternative of an independent Ulster were to be adopted. Moreover, whatever the politicians may think, opinion surveys and common observation both suggest that there is widespread public support for some form of integration with Britain.

This is a settlement, however, for which the initiative will never come from Ulster. It starts from the assumption that Ulster's troubles cannot be ended unless her divisions can be absorbed into a wider context than Ulster herself. If, of course, the Convention were to evolve a system of regional government based on power-sharing and commanding the genuine support of the vast majority, and of all whose support is essential to its operation, everything in the garden would be beautiful. The British Government could heave a huge sigh of relief and lavish congratulations on itself for its foresight and pertinacity. But this is not likely to happen. If by some miracle it did, the explanation could only be that the Convention politicians had examined the alternatives rationally and decided that even power-sharing was preferable to them. At present, however, no clear alternatives have been presented to them. The British are content with veiled threats of financial and military desertion which terrify only those whom it should be concerned to encourage.

The proper course is surely for the British Government to set out without further delay—calmly, rationally and exhaustively—what the alternatives are. These will turn out in the end to be either an independent Ulster, with all the consequences listed in this chapter, or some species of integration as described here. If that choice were put to the vote, there can be little doubt that the qualified system of integration would win. The knowledge that Ulster might be confronted with such a choice would, if anything, tend to encourage rather than discourage the Convention from agreeing on its own proposals.

What then stops Britain from adopting this course? The traditional answer is that British politicians shrink from anything which might increase the Irish element in the Commons and put Irishmen once again in a position to dominate British politics. Twenty Ulstermen at Westminster, however, would be unlikely to have this effect, particularly at a time when the British political parties have developed so powerful an instinct for ganging up against their Ulster colleagues. It is not to be supposed either, as recent experience has shown, that even Protestant Ulstermen at Westminster can be assumed to be invariably on the Tory side. Although the Labour party is missing a glittering opportunity by not extending the hand of friendship to Ulster's Protestant working class, it is doubtful whether a modest increase in Ulster representation would greatly alter the balance of power at Westminster. If British politicians could liberate themselves from the absurd modern convention of supposing that a uniform system of franchise is essential to the functioning of Parliament; if they would consent to have Ulster MPs elected by proportional representation as the Convention will be elected, then this particular objection could be wholly removed. If Parliament had the sense and justice to adopt PR for the whole of the United Kingdom, the objection would not exist at all.

In reality, the British shrinking from total integration—although it is the only settlement which now stands the smallest chance of success—arises from a deep-set but unconfessed British wish (prevalent among the politicians rather than the public) to be rid of Ulster altogether. In particular and at present, it springs from the knowledge that whoever else may accept integration the Provisional IRA certainly will not. Undoubtedly,

143

the adoption of this policy would bring the Provisionals back into action in Britain as well as in Ulster. The only possibly viable alternative policy, however—independence plus partition—would also almost certainly have the effect of involving Britain in further military conflict. The only way to make sure of avoiding such conflict would be instant and unconditional withdrawal, a course which British politicians, for the most part, also reject in horror.

If the conflict is to go on, the need is to ensure that it should be conducted in the most favourable conditions for Britain. That presupposes a policy likely to elicit the greatest popular support in Ulster, and there are solid arguments for supposing that this is integration on the kind of terms described here. Given the measure of unity which this policy could generate, the IRA, unless allowed to refresh itself by a prolonged armistice, would no longer be a particularly daunting enemy.

Epilogue

Some lessons of general application may be derived from this bitter story. It is an extraordinarily vivid illustration of the dangers of 'establishment politics', of what happens when a nation's political leaders are wholly out of touch with the senti-ments and prejudices of the people.

The British Government, for example, throughout these five years has been totally indifferent to one glaring truth about the state of British public feeling on the subject of Ulster. At almost any time during this period it would have been possible to achieve massive popular support in this country for a policy aimed, with almost complete ruthlessness, at the destruction of the IRA. It would have been equally possible to achieve substantial British support for a policy of total withdrawal based on the proposition that the affairs of Ulster were those of a distant and alien people in whose preservation the British had no national interest. In the event, successive British governments have secured the reluctant and bewildered acquiescence of the elec-torate in an enormous military commitment carried out nobly and efficiently by the Army, but under the gravest political restraints and with no clearly defined and consistent political objective. When a policy, however vague, is jointly undertaken by both major political parties in Britain, the public, for a long time at least, will dumbly acquiesce in its pursuit. If this war were to be swiftly and efficiently won, it would have been necessary to elicit some popular enthusiasm on its behalf: not the smallest attempt has ever been made to do this.

Although governments have been able to conduct this cam-paign with almost no regard to the feelings and wishes of the electorate, they have constantly pleaded popular prejudice as an excuse for waging it ineffectually. Every proposal for decisive action in Ulster has been met by the argument that the British electorate would not stand for it: nothing could be further from the truth. The British electorate has no natural sympathy for rebellion. It is not particularly moved by student demonstrations and protests in favour of 'civil rights' either. It has no natural inclination to support subversion. The political establishment in Britain, however, has played its game according to its own rules, the chief of which presupposes an electorate with an unconquerable aversion to the exercise of power.

Successive British governments in their handling of Ulster have failed to establish any *rapport* with the British electorate on the subject. They have failed even more staggeringly to show any grasp of public feeling in Ulster. Public opinion in Ulster, however, is not a particularly mysterious thing. The people there have not reacted—save in respect of their greater endurance— very differently from any other people to the experience of constant guerilla attack. The failure to understand what this would ultimately do to the Protestant population was wholly inexcusable. The most vivid illustration of the dangers of 'establishment politics' is provided, however, by the fate of moderate Ulster politicians, and more particularly by that of Mr Brian Faulkner. His political talents are outstanding and his patriotism is beyond reproach, and he started his career with one immense advantage over almost all his political rivals in Ulster—an unfailing sensitivity to the feelings of the Ulster Protestant majority. He was never merely the instrument of that majority. For years, he succeeded in cajoling and directing it into sane courses, many of which were utterly repugnant to its prejudices. By virtue of the confidence which he enjoyed, and the skill with which he put it to use, he held, more than any other man, the key to an enduring settlement in Ulster. He operated, however, under one overwhelming disadvantage—the final dependence of Ulster upon the support of British governments. In his efforts to maintain that support, he allowed himself to become ever more isolated from his own popular support. By contagion, he adopted a British style of politics which left him bereft and, in the end, useless even as an instrument of British policy.

In Britain, part of the establishment myth is that it is impossible for government to win an urban guerilla war. If this is true, the outlook for the civilized world is extremely poor, for undoubtedly most countries in the Western world may now expect to be confronted with the sort of challenge which has arisen in Ulster. What Ulster has proved, however, is that it is impossible for government to win a guerilla war if at the outset it discards all its most useful weapons. A vast army presence is no substitute, for example, for auxiliary police forces with intimate local knowledge and close contact with the population. The Loyalist strike of 1974 also vividly illustrated the power of industrial action for political ends when the authorities are wholly unprepared for such a challenge. A close study of its course would be of the greatest possible relevance to British politics.

Obsessed by the belief that the main object of government, when confronted by a revolutionary movement, must be to detach potential moderates from the support of that movement, British politicians were always ready to make concessions at the expense of security in Ulster in the belief that by so doing they would achieve that end. This belief has repeatedly been proved false. The concessions have increased the power of the rebels to intimidate, and conferred ever-growing prestige on them. As a result, they have gathered more support. All revolutionary movements take care to equip themselves with the protection of apparently moderate political movements, like the Civil Rights Movement and the SDLP in Ulster, which can be used to extort valuable concessions from democratic governments anxious to 'win over' the uncommitted part of the population. What is essential to defeating a revolution, however, is the will to victory. In most such crises, the government starts with an effective monopoly of public force. Only the knowledge that this force will, if necessary, be thoroughly used can induce in the rebels the despair which is a necessary condition of their defeat. Had Britain concentrated singlemindedly on producing that despair in the IRA, the battle in Ulster would now be over.

Much play has been made with the theme that it is impossible for a government to suppress rebellion under the constant scrutiny of the media. That is not true. What is true is that the liberal bias of the media will always operate against the interests of authority, and that journalists and television commentators often become the unwitting agents of revolutionary propaganda. The answer to this threat is not censorship or suppression but effective exposition of the reasons for government action. The notion that it is necessary to use brute force to meet brute force is by no means shocking to the minds of ordinary citizens. The fact that mistakes can be made and crimes committed in the course of military and police action, but that these mistakes and crimes do not invalidate the case for such action, is not difficult for the ordinary intellect to grasp. It is a fact, however, on which democratic governments will never rely. They play into the hands of their enemies by accepting the proposition that if the police or the Army is ever at fault, an indestructible case has been established for changing the policy which the police and the Army are being employed to enforce. No more convincing illustration of this truth can be found than 'Bloody Sunday' and the political consequences it produced.

One lesson, however, emerges more clearly than any other from the British experience in Ulster since 1968. It is the desperate danger of hand-to-mouth politics, of the assumption that the clear analysis of broad political choices and the attempt to estimate the consequences which will follow from them is an academic activity with no bearing on practical politics. British empiricism is an infinitely valuable political style, but it does not imply a total suspension of reason. Thinking is a necessary part of statecraft. The real explanation for the failure of British policy in Ulster since 1968 is that those responsible for that policy have fallen far short of the standards of sensible mediocrity for which the British are traditionally supposed to look in their statesmen.

Postscript
On 1 May the Convention elections yielded the expected Loyalist victory and inflicted further humiliations on those parties which claimed to represent the Centre. The most important development since these pages went to press, however, has been Mr Rees's announcement, on 24 July, of the Government's hope that it will be possible to release all detainees by Christmas. This announcement, a week after the brutal and planned murder of four UK soldiers by the IRA, and following closely on yet another characteristically inflexible statement of IRA war aims, has greatly increased the doubts about the aims of the present Government's policy expressed earlier in this book. In Ulster in particular, it has prompted a crucial question: is it conceivable, even allowing for the eccentricities of British statesmanship, that a government which intended to preserve the Union in defiance of the IRA would be calmly contemplating the release of over two hundred terrorists, many of them dangerous and highly skilled fighters, in spite of the mounting evidence that the IRA is preparing for a resumption of hostilities on both sides of the Irish Sea? Does this move lend support to the claim of the Reverent William Arlow, one of the Protestant clergymen who took part in the

exploratory discussions with the Provos at Feakle, that the British Government has already made a secret agreement to withdraw from Ulster if the Convention fails to produce a constitution satisfactory to British requirements?

Past experience has not encouraged unqualified acceptance of the Government's denials on this point. Whatever the truth of the matter, one thing is certain: mounting anxieties about British intentions have greatly strengthened throughout Ulster what, until recently, was the view of a small minority—that the Province's future might best be assured by total, or nearly total, independence of the United Kingdom.

To the Loyalists, including many Official Unionists, the British presence in Ulster is increasingly identified with weak security policies and treacherous diplomacy. Many of them ask whether it would not be better to sacrifice the cherished connection altogether so that the majority might itself be free to stamp out Republican terrorism. The SDLP itself is just as panic-stricken by the general trend of Mr Rees's policy. Some of its members at least are beginning to reason thus: if Britain is really bent on withdrawal, would it not be wiser to come to terms with the loyalists within the framework of an independent Ulster than to cling to the vanishing hope that the British will, in the last resort, be ready to discharge their obligations to the Catholic minority even at the cost of exposing themselves to renewed IRA attack? Many believe that that question lies behind the tentative negotiations which have already started between the UUUC (United Ulster Unionist Coalition) and the SDLP.

The Dublin Government, which is now far more hostile to the IRA than is the British Government, and has recently demonstrated this hostility by arresting David O'Connell, the Provos' Chief of Staff, also looks with mounting apprehension on the prospect of British withdrawal.

Significantly, Labour politicians in Britain and British civil servants concerned with Ulster increasingly dwell (with ill-concealed satisfaction) on what they are pleased to describe as the growing power of 'Ulster nationalism'. There should be no mistake, however, on this point: what in Westminster and Whitehall is dignified as Ulster nationalism is nothing more nor less than a growing suspicion that Britain intends to abandon Ulster. Could it be that that suspicion is being deliberately fostered by the British Government in the hope that it will lead to some sort of negotiated independence which would be accepted in despair by

Ulster's political parties, and would also temporarily satisfy the IRA? The horrific consequences of such a settlement have already been indicated in this book. It is in the light of them that Mr Rees's policy should now be considered by Parliament and the electorate.

The alternative to that policy is a bold reassertion of Britain's readiness to maintain the Union at the cost of extending direct rule and accompanying it with proper arrangements for Ulster's representation at Westminster and the restoration of effective local government in the Province. That such proposals, however unpopular they might at first be with Ulster politicians, would command substantial support among both communities in the Province, and evoke at least a subdued sigh of relief from Dublin, cannot be doubted. But the sands are running out. If Britain maintains her present policy of singularly unmasterful inactivity until deadlock is reached at the Convention, positions in Ulster will have become too rigid to be affected by anything that may come from Whitehall.

Meanwhile, the chief brunt of all this confusion and suspense continues to be borne by the security forces in Ulster. With steadfastness and restraint, they carry out, in the face of ever-mounting difficulties, a policy which lacks purpose and direction and which exposes them to constant insult and danger. Hampered though they be by inept political direction, their skill and valour remain the only barrier between Ulster and anarchy, and between Britain and the most dishonourable surrender in her history.

Appendix I

Principal dates relative to British policy in Ulster since 1969

28 April 1969	Resignation of Captain Terence O'Neill as Prime Minister of Ulster
1 May 1969	Appointment of Major James Chichester-Clark as Prime Minister of Ulster
13 August 1969	British Government despatches troops to Londonderry
15 August 1969	British Government despatches troops to Belfast
20 August 1969	Joint 'Downing Street' declaration by British and Northern Irish Governments on control of security in Northern Ireland and proposed political reforms there
20 March 1971	Major James Chichester-Clark resigns as Prime Minister of Ulster
23 March 1971	Brian Faulkner appointed as Prime Minister of Ulster
16 July 1971	Social Democratic and Labour party (Catholic Opposition) withdraw from Stormont Parliament in protest against the British Government's refusal to hold an independent inquiry into two deaths in Londonderry in the course of a riot
9 August 1971	Detention and internment without trial reactivated in Northern Ireland
31 January 1972 ('Bloody Sunday')	Thirteen people killed in the course of Army action arising from a riot in Londonderry
25 March 1972	British Government announces Direct Rule for Ulster
26 June 1972	Provisional IRA announces ceasefire. Fourteen days later Provisional IRA announces end of ceasefire
31 July 1972	Operation 'Motorman' brings Army back into the 'no-go' areas
21 March 1973	British Government publishes White Paper on constitutional future of Northern Ireland
28 June 1973	Northern Irish Assembly elected under the terms of a new constitution Act
22 October 1973	A power-sharing Executive designate appointed in Northern Ireland
9 December 1973	Sunningdale agreement on the future relationship between Northern and Southern Ireland following a conference between representatives of the British and Southern Irish Governments and the parties composing the Executive designate in Ulster
28 February 1974	Westminster General Election produces a powerful swing to 'Loyalists' in Ulster
16–30 May 1974	A general strike in Ulster against Sunningdale agreement and power-sharing Executive
20 November 1974	British Government White Paper announces decision to hold elections in Northern Ireland for a convention to make proposals for a future constitutional settlement
22 December 1974	IRA begins ceasefire
16 January 1975	Ceasefire ends
10 February 1975	Ceasefire renewed
1 May 1975	Convention elections

Appendix II

Toll of Violence

TABLE I. DEATHS RESULTING FROM TERRORIST ACTIVITIES

	1969	1970	1971	1972	1973	1974	1975*	Total
Civilians	12	23	114	322	170	166	36	**857**
Army	—	—	43	103	58	28	2	**233**
RUC	1	2	11	14	10	12	2	**51**
UDR	—	—	5	25	9	7	—	**46**
RUCR	—	—	—	3	3	3	—	**10**
Total	**13**	**25**	**173**	**467**	**250**	**216**	**40**	**1,197**

TABLE II. INJURIES

		1969	1970	1971	1972	1973	1974	1975*	Total
RUC		711	191	317	466	291	235	20	**2,231**
Army and UDR		22†	99	279	707	548	483	25	**2,163**
Civilians		NA*	—	1,799	3,998	1,812	1,680	188	**9,477**
Total	379	733	290	2,395	5,171	2,651	2,398	233	**13,871**

TABLE III. EXPLOSIONS

1969	1970	1971	1972	1973	1974	1975*
8	155	1,033	1,495	1,007	669	78

TABLE IV. TARRINGS-AND-FEATHERINGS

1969	1970	1971	1972	1973	1974	1975*
—	—	27	28	6	16	6

TABLE V. ATTACKS ON POLICE STATIONS

1969	1970	1971	1972	1973	1974	1975*
28	31	261	269	212	155	22

* 1975 until March 31
† Figure includes injuries to Ulster Defence Regiment members
NA* not available

Appendix III

Movement of opinion in Northern Ireland as shown by election results in 1973 and 1974

TABLE I. ASSEMBLY ELECTIONS FOR 1973

	Percentage of votes cast
Pro Power-sharing	
Unionists	26·3
Alliance	9·3
NILP	2·7
SDLP	22·2
Total	**60·5**
Anti Power-sharing	
Unionists	11·6
'Loyalists'	23·4
Total	**35·0**
Others	
Republican Clubs	1·9
Independents	2·6
Total	**4·5**

TABLE II. GENERAL ELECTIONS OF 1974

	Percentage of votes cast	
	February	October
Pro Power-sharing		
UPNI	13·1	3·1
Alliance	3·2	6·3
NILP	2·4	1·6
SDLP	22·4	21·9
Anti Power-sharing		
UUUC	51·1	58·0
Others	7·8	9·1

Appendix IV

The cost of Northern Ireland

The gap between Northern Ireland's approved expenditure and what Northern Ireland's own tax yields, other revenue sources, and loans from the United Kingdom National Loans Fund can contribute has been increasing. This gap is covered by a subvention from United Kingdom Government funds.

TABLE I.

					£ million			
	1966 –67	1967 –68	1968 –69	1969 –70	1970 –71	1971 –72	1972 –73	1973 –74
Social services (including Health until 1971–72)	10	10	19	16	24	40	45	31
Health services	—	—	—	—	—	20	25	15
Regional Employment Premium	—	4	9	10	11	11	11	8
Remoteness Grant (Agriculture)	2	2	2	2	2	2	2	2
Agricultural subsidies paid by Ministry of Agriculture, Fisheries and Food	25	30	31	31	37	31	25	30
National Insurance	15	17	13	15	14	22	22	30
Grant-in-Aid	—	—	—	—	—	—	51	175
Northern Ireland Office reserved services	—	—	—	—	—	—	—	21
Refund of VAT	—	—	—	—	—	—	—	1
Total Payments	52	63	74	74	88	126	181	313

Table II shows the additional expense to the United Kingdom defence budget arising from operations in Northern Ireland since 1969. In 1973–74 (the last year for which figures are available) the part of the defence expenditure directly attributable to the Northern Ireland operation was only £33 million. Thus, the chief burden of the Northern Ireland campaign on Britain may fairly be said to be strategic rather than financial. It consists in the diversion of troops from other possible areas of employment. At present the strength of the United Kingdom Army in Ulster is approximately 14,000. At its peak, in July 1972, it was approximately 21,000.

TABLE II. ADDITIONAL COST TO UK DEFENCE BUDGET OF NORTHERN IRELAND MILITARY OPERATIONS

1969–70	1970–71	1971–72	1972–73	1973–74
1·5	6·5	14·3	29·0	33·0